Beyond Failure

A Journey to Self

Connie Lynne

Author of
"Inner Strength Guide"

Copyright © 2015 by Connie Lynne

All quotations remain the intellectual property of their respective originators. The author does not assert any claim of copyright for individual quotations. All use of quotations is done under the fair use copyright principal.

Library and Archives Canada Cataloguing in Publication

Lynne, Connie, 1965-

Beyond Failure /Connie Lynne

Necessity4Failure enterprises
www.necessity4failure.com

May the thoughts and insights written within these pages help alter any of your negative perceptions of failure.

May this book also grant you the freedom to be open with yourself, and others, so that you may gain the required strength and endurance to transform your life.

May these reflections guide you in the direction that only YOU are destined to follow.

"It is not the critic who counts, not the man who points out how the strong man stumbled, or where the doer of deeds could have done better. The credit belongs to the man who is actually in the arena, whose face is marred by dust and sweat and blood, who strives valiantly, who errs and comes short again and again, who knows the great enthusiasms, the great devotions, and spends himself in a worthy cause, who at best knows achievement and who at the worst if he fails at least fails while daring greatly so that his place shall never be with those cold and timid souls who know neither victory nor defeat."

~ Theodore Roosevelt

Table of Content

Preface	1
Introduction to Failure	4
Disclosure	5
Failure Revealed	6
My Challenge	8
Perceptions	17
Desperate Times	24
Veils of Pretense	33
Bubble of Denial	41
Authenticity	46
Core Values	52
Transparency	57
Excommunicated	63
Reality Check	67
Growth through Failure	76
Learning Process	77
Recognizing Abilities	78
Failing to use Intuition	81
Self Confidence	86
Reprogramming	88
Mistaken Identity	90
Not Guilty	98
Through The Process	101

Love Forever	102
Beauty within Ashes	111
Facing Reality	116
Other People's Grief	119
The Help that Harms	121
Letting Go	130
Reality vs. Perception	136
Avoiding Emotions	139
In the Eye of the Storm	144
Illusions	149
Within the Darkness	151
Acceptance	157
Awareness	159
Root Cause	161
Dream	164
Footnote for the Ego	167
Gratitude for Everything	168
A Tiny Bit of my Gratitude List:	169
Trial and Error	172
Great Examples of Failure	177
Insights on Failure	183

Preface

I have FELT LIKE A FAILURE most of my life. Even as a child, like many children, I felt alone in my humiliation. I didn't want to accept what, deep down, I knew to be true: That I was flawed.

What exactly was I doing that kept me locked in my shameful prison? I needed to know, what I did not know. And thus, began my transformational journey.

As I stumbled forward, my ignorance combined with my false assumptions and self-doubt prolonged my painful pursuit.

I used the light of Truth to guide me, however, this proved to be a challenge, which I will elaborate on throughout these pages. The reflection of light had to come from within me, not from outside of me.

When I began questioning my self-imposed labels, transformation followed. What appeared to be my largest stumbling blocks were, in fact, my future stepping stones. Within the rubble of my failures I found what I was seeking. Failure was not what I thought!

My journey brought me to a crossroad. I found myself at a junction where I could either continue in my futility or change my paradigm. In my weakness, overwhelmed by the burden of my failures, I gave up. In the depths of my despair, shrouded in darkness, I surrendered.

No longer could I pretend to know what I did not know. Everything around me, everything in my experience, was a reflection of what I had been focusing on. I had been the author of my own predicament. I had mistakenly smothered my own success. Freedom from failure was now a reality. Liberated, I embraced my vulnerability and a miracle began to unfold.

Within these pages are some of the more memorable lessons, insights, and understandings I have gained through close examination of my own personal setbacks.

My experiences have shown me, no matter how different we are, and how different our opinions may seem, people respond similarly to certain situations, failure included.

As we journey together, it is vital that you value and appreciate our magnificent character differences as well as our similarities. I would like to stress the importance of your individual perspective while you read through these pages.

Warning: This book is biased. It is biased because we are all biased. We justify our actions as we form our opinions, thoughts and ideals.

We are perfectly imperfect: Your exceptional nature is one of your many attributes that you were born to honour and protect. If you do not embrace your uniqueness, you subconsciously de-value yourself. It takes courage to grow up and be who you really are.

As you grow through life, you will be bombarded with

advice: Other people's concepts of who you should or should not be. In recognition of this, remain mindful of what, or who, you allow to direct you.

There is much good to be had from the guidance of others, including your own, however, in the pursuit of knowledge, be careful not to lose your essential core; your true essence.

No one can afford to wander around blindly accepting someone else's absolute Truth just because it has been stated as such. What is completely relevant to one might not be appropriate for another, depending on the focus or goal at that particular time.

Since we are meant to be individuals, there is no one set paths for everyone. In fact, there are limitless passages. Your personal path will provide its own life lessons, as it already has. With that said, we also need to appreciate that we can learn a lot from others.

As you stay true to your own specific desires, you can be more open to new ideas. The liberating thing about this is: when you focus on your strengths and accept your weaknesses, you won't feel as intimidated by other people's opinions. You can simply decipher what is useful for you and disregard the things that do not pertain to your specific life goals and circumstances … Simple as that!

"Believe nothing, no matter where you read it, or who said it, no matter if I have said it, unless it agrees with your own reason and your own common sense."

~ Buddha

Introduction to Failure

It's been said, *"Success has a thousand fathers and failure is but an orphan."*

I'm here to plead on behalf of this abandoned orphan. My desire is to prove that when you adopt failure you will grow beyond your wildest dreams.

Throughout these pages I'm going to reveal to you why failure is a tool that we cannot live without. Like an orphan, we as a society have rejected failure without realizing the ramifications of this action.

Mistakes, setbacks and misfortunes are unavoidable and unfortunately, 'stuff' happens to everyone. I can assure you that the benefit of adopting failure well outweighs the cost. By changing your attitude about failure, you will see your life transform in unimaginable ways.

Acknowledge your failures. Allow them to strengthen you. They will help you grow more resilient as you move towards your unlimited potential.

"Let a person radically alter his thoughts, and he will be astonished at the rapid transformation it will effect in the material conditions of his life."

~ James Allen

Disclosure

Before we begin, I need to make a confession.

Initially, when I began writing this, I felt the need to present myself as more articulate than I felt I was. I started writing with elaborations and bombastic words that I was not accustomed to using. I added some garble, expanding on things I thought the educated would deem imperative to my topic. I was trying to portray myself as this incredible writer in the hope that I would impress you, my reader; why I, Connie Lynne was important enough to write this book.

Needless to say, my initial desire to be perfect, in relaying my imperfection, did not bring out my best self. Midway through my writing, I allowed myself to surface through these pages. Because of this, I found it necessary to re-write the majority of this book, so I could remain true to my initial purpose. I needed to be brutally honest, and speak one-on-one with you, exposing the authentic me. The process I have allowed this project to take has been incredibly liberating. Truth be told, I don't believe I would have had the courage to write this book if it was not about failure.

Sure, there are a LOT of success books out there. But what seems to have been forgotten is that success is built upon the shoulders of past failure. This book is not strictly about failure, although I will reference failure many times. Toward the end, if you can appreciate it, you will discover everything in life involves failure.

Failure Revealed

Before revealing myself in the more intimate terms necessary, I would like to state an important fact: I would not give up one part of my life for all I have become through it. Perhaps it may have been nice to have learned my lessons more quickly. That way, I could have been at this point in my life sooner; however, life doesn't seem to reveal itself before we are ready.

How we perceive any given circumstance can distort our interpretation of a situation. The following thoughts and reflections are based on my own perceptions. I am humbled and sincerely honoured to reveal the insights I have obtained through years of studying, personal development, combined with my own colourful journey.

There is much knowledge hidden within our unpleasant experiences. When we become aware of that therapeutic insight, we gain the ability to be more relaxed within the process of failure, accepting its guidance within our journey. Through this acceptance, we increase the speed of our learning because we are no longer fighting the process.

In order to grow through any challenging life experience, it is important to remember: We cannot know everything. It is impossible to comprehend all that happens around us. When we are open to seeing what we may not have seen, our potential for growth increases enormously. As such, it is important to refrain from any negative judgement.

Depending on your perception of a negative experience, you will either grow, building on the new found knowledge, or you will stay blind to the insight within it, remaining stuck. Our moments of perceived failure can either hinder our growth, or guide us to unlimited knowledge. Which one will you choose?

When you train yourself to see the bigger picture within a setback you gain the clarity needed to receive the value of the lesson. Gaining acceptance of your mistakes and setbacks makes it easier to acknowledge the need for change.

When you fail you can either re-try until you are successful, or accept that what you were attempting to do is not what you were meant to be doing. In either case, you are taking the failure as a slight directional shift as you continue on your personal journey.

"You know better, you do better!"

~ Grandma

My Challenge

My area of expertise is something the world refers to as "failure". Within these pages, I will provide you a sampling of the insights I have gained through my constant exposure to them. To clarify, I am not revealing my failures to impress you, isn't that a bizarre statement? But rather impress upon you the need for failure.

Being an expert in this field might not sound like the most distinguished label one could acknowledge. However, throughout my numerous failings I have learned countless things about this particular process that has, in fact, helped me grow stronger. Even now, as I consider those important life altering blunders, setbacks and mistakes, I become aware of even more wisdom that can be extracted from those encounters.

My intention is to take the embarrassment out of the failure experience. My desire is that my openness will help you accept your own failures. Imperfections are a part of life. Wouldn't it be a lot easier to deal with our own failures, the past and our inevitable future ones, knowing we are not alone? We all make mistakes. We all fail!

The seemingly random failures I have chosen to share are just a few from my vast collection. For whatever reason, these particular ones have remained clear within my memory, preserving the specific details of those moments in time. Of course, I am not unique in this way. We all have memories that are as pure and vivid as if they had taken place but a moment ago.

I invite you to join with me as we travel back in time, through some of my more colourful failures. Within this book you will share many of the painful moments of my life.

The stories will not be in order due to how our memories jump around from one thought to the next.

Throughout the course of this book, you will get to know me fairly well, but you will get to know yourself even better. My goal is that you question your concepts. That you find comfort in a world that often has none. Don't be afraid to challenge what is written in this book. On the other hand, while reading, keep an open mind and consider my shared experiences with yours.

If you allow yourself to identify with my experiences, you will be drawn back to your own. I encourage you to flow through your own memories and embrace your past with the detachment that time provides. Allow yourself to see your past 'life experiences' as valuable lessons guiding you to your next level of learning. What did the lesson hold within it? What altered your direction? How did it influence your eventual path?

As you become more comfortable with your past mistakes, you are more likely to anticipate foreseeable future ones. In doing this, you will not have to repeat past lessons.

Let us now move forward, my memories sharing with yours, as we embark on a journey to change how we view our embarrassments and setbacks from my world… to yours.

Limiting my possibilities

Nervously I walked up the familiar stairs and entered through one of the heavy glass entrance doors. My feelings were mixed as to what I was about to do. Part of me despised this place for the constant reminder it gave me regarding my utter stupidity and ignorance. On the other hand, this was a place of refuge from my overwhelming responsibilities at home.

My instructions were clear. I was to head straight to my locker. Be fast and focused. Empty out my contents. Return immediately back to the front of the school where the car would be waiting.

This should only take a moment, I thought to myself as my fingers slipped on the combination lock. Fear of being caught was making an easy task next to impossible.

I paused for a moment to try to remember the sequence of my locker combination. My thoughts danced in slow motion. The sound of a door slamming jerked me back into the moment. I looked around; there was no one in the hallways.

Was I really doing this? My hands were sweating; it was hard to stay focused on those little numbers. After what seemed to be eternity…click…it was open.

I clumsily pushed the books and binders into my backpack, making sure not to take my locker partner's things. My thoughts drifted for a moment to what she would think when she discovered that I had just disappeared.

School was in session. I had been absent for several days and yet, as far as I knew, no one had enquired about my whereabouts. No time to think. I needed to get out of there before I was seen.

Relieved to have completed my mission, I was almost free. Free from the life I could not please. Free of the constant reminder of my inadequacies. Now, at the tender age of thirteen, my years of formal education were closing.

I was not aware of the impact this life altering decision would have on my future. Unknown to me, I was heading towards the lessons that needed to be endured and would still have to be taught through the failures looming in my future.

How did I get to this point?

In order to understand my relationship with failure we are going to have to start at the very beginning...

I was the first twin born in the newly developed town of Pinawa, Manitoba. With this first place position you would think that I would have been a natural for success (keep in mind, if that had been the case you would not be reading this book).Consequently, I hold my *first place* title with great pride.

My brother, on the other hand, refused to be born in the same town as his twin sister (me), so he and my parents took the next available ambulance out of there, leaving me to fend on my own with the doctors, nurses and hospital staff.

Just shy of eight hours later, my twin brother, Richard, was born in the city of Winnipeg, 114 km away.

As a result of my successful battle to get out of the womb first, Richard was born with a lack of oxygen and entered this world blue (don't worry, he has since regained his colour).

I state, rather jealously, that he has always had an extremely high IQ. I shudder to think what type of genius he could have been if he had received a bit more of that precious oxygen of which he was initially deprived.

Clearly my parents must have thought things were too easy with our slightly older brother James, my twin brother Richard and myself, so they quickly provided us a sister, Jacquie less than a year later. This means, three of us siblings are the same age for a few weeks every year.

My Mom was only twenty one and already had four children, my Dad, not much older.

Obviously my parents were enjoying their alone time. However, we will not go into more detail on that because these are my parents and as we all know…parents don't do that.

* * * *

My difficulties started early and so did my feelings of failure. I struggled in my early years with just the basics, like breathing. Life was good in my tiny world, unless someone outside my immediate family dared to look at me, or try to talk to me.

If strangers would attempt to break my illusion of solitude and look at me, or (heaven forbid!) try to talk to me, I'd start crying. This invariably started a chain reaction. I would start to cry, forget to breathe and then proceed to black out; a cycle that concerned everyone, particularly my parents.

People around me learned early to just leave me in my delusional bubble without distractions.

As I got older, everyone accepted the basic ground

rule: *Don't look at her!*

The times when I was forced to venture away from the security of my home, I would cling to my mother's leg, not daring to look away from the ground which provided me with the illusion that the outside world was not around me. In my bubble of denial, I was safe.

At the end of a day, my parents would try to cuddle and connect with me, but that did not work for me. I was a rigid 'need-my-space' type child. I preferred not to be constrained unless the need for security deemed it necessary, then (and only then!) would I use their laps to ward off the outside world.

Quite frankly, I'm not sure how I survived the transition from home to kindergarten. I was traumatized at the very thought of having to face a world which I was in absolute denial over.

My beginning school years are more blurred than my earlier pre-kindergarten years, probably because I could not accept that reality, and so for me, it did not exist.

The school system, combined with my parents, felt it would be in my best interest for me to be placed into a 'special' class.

I certainly didn't feel like a failure at this time. Not comparing myself with others, I wasn't aware of the standards or expectations, nor where I fell within those categories.

My siblings were extremely jealous of my cushy placement and in turn, this made me happy; I was 'special'. With my new label of learning disabled, I continued with the educational process.

A few obvious abnormalities led to my special label. I had a speech impediment and could not say my Rr's nor could I hear if I'd said them correctly (this was an extra difficult challenge having a twin brother named Richard).

On top of that, due to my painfully shy and timid behaviour, I'd not developed the necessary social skills that could help me interact with my peers. And of course, the most obvious abnormality of the bunch was the mastery of that whole breathing, walking, talking thing. It was expected that I should be able to perform all of those simultaneously as the world looked on appeared like insanity! (It's amazing that they didn't ask me to walk on water).

During this time, I was being dragged from one doctor to another to see what was wrong with me. I remember one particular doctor, an ears, nose, and throat specialist, who took an eternity probing, pulling, and staring into my mouth. He finally concluded my tongue was too short. He went so far as to measure it (Where does the tongue start anyway?). I had doctors roaming around in my ears because of some inner ear thing? One doctor kept pushing into my stomach till it hurt making me cry.

Believe it or not, I didn't feel abnormally abnormal. I had not yet put two and two together, feeling I was just 'me'. Throughout all these struggles, amazingly, I remained fairly content and happy.

I didn't understand the need everyone seemed to have to pull me out of my comfortable solitary bubble of existence. Why didn't everyone just leave me alone? I was determined to live my life in this safe bubble of denial. I didn't know what this 'normal' was that people spoke of. I didn't know I was a failure…yet!

The fateful day I remember being introduced to failure was a bitterly dark, cold, blustery day (Okay, I'm not really sure if the sun was shining or if the wind was indeed blowing, but to me, and my memory thereafter, it became a dark, cold, and blustery day).

The classroom I attended was delightfully relaxing. We didn't really have to work and, as I look back, no negative words were ever spoken. All I had to do all day long was to draw or print fascinating stories. When my self-directed projects were completed, I would excitedly bounce to the front of the classroom and proudly show Mr. Fast, my teacher, my accomplishments. He'd look up from his work and nod in approval. I'd grin from ear to ear and rush back to my desk to work on my next masterpiece.

A few days each week someone would come and get me from my special class to go to my *'extra special'* class: speech therapy. *Looking back, I can see that they were totally disrupting my creative process.*

As it became customary, they would appear at the door and motion for me to follow. I'd pull myself awkwardly from my desk as though I was about to be unfairly punished. Not making eye contact, I'd stare intently down at the floor as I was escorted to the trailer parked outside the school where these classes were held.

The process was always a duplicate of the previous session. I would be expected to repeat various sounds spoken by the instructor. I desperately wanted to echo back the sound they created. *If I could just make everyone happy and simply articulate what they wanted me to say in the exact manner that they regarded as accurate, the world would surely be a perfect place.*

After many, many sessions of this monotony, at long last, I did it! I was certain that I'd repeated the sound exactly as it should've sounded, as if, it had been spoken straight from…God himself!

So positive that I had gotten it this time, I proudly looked up from my gaze on the floor to see, to my dismay, them shaking their heads in utter frustration. Choking back tears of disappointment, I once again forgot to breathe and lost consciousness.

As I came to, I overheard how hopeless I was and how *this little girl was simply not going to get it.* I don't remember their exact words but I do remember the feeling of absolute failure. I was devastated and wanted to completely disappear. As they walked me back to my classroom, I found myself unable to face my world at all. Unable to muddle through my mind what had just happened, I wanted to become invisible.

After I was dropped off at my classroom I crawled under one of the desks in the corner of the room in hopes no one would notice me. However, the substitute teacher looked intently in my direction from the other side of the room and requested firmly, "Little boy, sit properly in your desk, not under it." Insult to injury. "I'm not a boy", I whimpered.

* * * *

The rest of that day is a bit of a blur, but one thing I do recall... I did not give up my spot under the safety of that desk willingly.

"There is nothing either good or bad, but thinking makes it so."
~ William Shakespeare

Perceptions

This is a good time to reflect on perception. I assumed because the people around me were getting frustrated with my lack of progress, I had failed. Not learning the "normal" way added to my database of stored information that I was subconsciously collecting about myself. I could not remain in my bubble of denial anymore. All the facts were in and they added up to:

Me = Failure!

In our early years especially, our perception of what others say or think about us can distort our view of ourselves. When we believe what other people are thinking or saying about us, our own beliefs begin to change, changing who we are. This, unfortunately, creates a ripple effect by making us question ourselves. This can make us turn against ourselves.

Our self-image is based upon our comparison of ourselves and others. Based on this, we tend to label ourselves as either good or bad. When we allow labels to define our self-image, we become more susceptible to alter the Truth of who we are. Unfortunately, when we accept a label as tragic as failure, the added pressure to be normal becomes all-consuming, and we often lose our positive self-identity.

We often base who we are on how we perceive others; what they do, what they don't do, what they think, and/or what they don't think. Because of our need to fit in and be 'normal', we think in comparisons. *How do I compare? Are they judging me?* This only creates distorted facts because our perception is built on what we assume others are thinking about us.

The reality is: You would get more accurate feedback going to an amusement park and looking into those distorted funhouse mirrors…a great illustration of trying to get an accurate view of who you are from someone else's personal perspective.

So, why do we feel that the response we receive (or rather *perceive*) from others is even close to an exact mirror image of Truth? When we believe this, we are allowing our self-images to be formed by outside responses. This almost certainly is not an accurate reflection. We are then no longer creating our Truth from within.

We become completely self-conscious of other people's observations of us; how they might be judging and/or categorizing us. In turn, we feel that we have failed when we are not initially successful when we try something new. Often, when we do not immediately achieve what we have set out to accomplish. We categorize ourselves as not capable. Then, in sheer embarrassment, we step back, humbly taking our place in what we see as an undesirable position: Failure.

This type of thinking happens within seconds. Without completely grasping the damaging effect of our own thoughts, we've labelled ourselves as failures. Whether true or not, our perception changes our view of reality and that ultimately changes our reality!

Another day in the life of a failure

One day my Dad decided this was going to be the day I was going to figure out, once and for all, the concept of fractions.

"This is easy stuff," he said as he placed a box on the table and motioned for me to sit down. "Look, it's as easy as pie," smirking as if he had just told a funny joke.

He started to pull out pieces of what appeared to possibly be a puzzle. The sections of the puzzle looked exactly like pieces of pie. *Wow! Dad had gone to the trouble to buy fraction puzzles that looked like a bunch of little pies.* I was excited! One of the puzzles particularly caught my undivided attention. *It was the most delicious looking scrumptious cherry pie I could have ever imagined the pleasure of enjoying.* My mouth was now watering, how deliciously real those pies appeared, *yum!* I could almost taste them.

My Dad noticed the cherry pie had caught my attention and gently placed the pieces of the puzzle in front of me. He slid out a piece that had been part of the whole pie and now was sitting separately.

He thoughtfully asked, "What is the fraction of this piece?"

Looking back, I can still see the fraction written on it which read, "¼".

Glancing at my Dad and then back to the pie I nervously stuttered, "It...it's...well...it's a delicious piece of cherry pie."

A little frustrated with my answer he asked me again, "What's the fraction?" He hinted to a coin that equals a quarter of a dollar and waited impatiently.

I looked at my Dad with my big eyes wide open, wanting so much to understand, hunting through my brain for the proper response. *This shouldn't be so hard*, I thought to myself. The pie looked incredibly delicious and I desperately didn't want to expose how dumb I was. I stammered a hopeful answer anticipating that by expressing how especially yummy that piece of cherry pie appeared I would somehow gain his approval.

In frustration, my Dad left the table not knowing what to do, or what to say to help me with my mental block. Sadly, I sat there feeling that I had once again failed.

The truth of the situation; I didn't comprehend the basic fundamentals of this mathematical formula.

When all we perceive is failure, choosing to prolong our embarrassment by continuing moving forward doesn't logically make sense for our mental survival. Feeling a situation is futile makes it tough, to say the least, to maintain a positive focus on what we are attempting to achieve.

Let's look over some of the basic fundamental things that society agrees we need to do to gain success. *What was I doing wrong?*

Set goals:

✓ My goal was to please my father and be able to understand the dreaded pie puzzle.

Positive mental attitude:

✓ I was open to learning and felt that I should be able to get it this time.

Intense desire:

✓ My desire was incredibly intense due to wanting to please my father, combined with needing to not be perceived as being brainless.

Plan and prepare:

✓ My life, as I saw it, prepared me for this education and this plan with the puzzle seemed fool proof.

Self-discipline:

✓ I was disciplined in sitting and listening and desperately wanting to learn.

Take action:

✓ I was in full can-do action mode. Sitting at the table working on the puzzle…taking action!

Persistence:

✓ Obviously this was not the first time I had tried to figure out fractions or we would never have had to resort to the pie puzzles.

As we go through this list it appears that I was following all of these success principles, but they were not supporting me in achieving the success that I was desperately seeking. I still failed.

What was I doing wrong?

Maybe, we need to look at this from another angle. *How had I come to be sitting at that table with the challenge of comprehending fractions? Had I advanced enough in my life to be at this next stage of learning?* All too often we forget where we have come from and what we have already accomplished in order to arrive at certain points in our lives.

Admittedly, I was still behind the other children in my age category. But in fairness to myself, I had already overcome many challenges. I had a pretty good handle on the walking, talking, breathing thing. Through much repetition, I was able to compose the sounds of the alphabet correctly, including my R's. I was only fainting when I'd hit my elbow or my knee; a natural reaction to that type of pain, don't you think? Okay, okay... maybe not natural to everyone, but still not unnatural to some.

In saying this, if we keep in mind and celebrate our past successes, we will remain encouraged to keep moving forward, building upon those successes. This way, when we inevitably stumble upon dilemmas that appear impossible and feel stuck, we have a reference point to fall back on. We can only view a situation as an opportunity for growth if we keep our focus on its reality. Choose to see how far you've come, rather than how far you have to go.

I strongly suggest that everyone keep a journal. This is an excellent way to express your personal frustrations while also providing opportunity for self-reflection.

A journal will record reflections of a situation that might have appeared futile, but after time, you see how it all worked out. Sometimes after writing down a specific problem, the answer will come to you and you'll be able to achieve what appeared to be the impossible: Success!!

I really like this quote below, as it reveals the possibilities and magical nature of a journal.

"These empty pages are your future, soon to become your past. They will read the most personal tale you shall ever find in a book."

~ Anonymous

Desperate Times

This next story occurred when I was about 7 years old. Sadly, I was not patting myself on the back for all of my modest successes, in fact, the complete opposite. I was kicking myself for all my obvious short comings. My inability to comprehend basic instructions combined with my negative judgment of myself seemed to pull me deeper into feelings of desperation.

The best way to describe my mental state at this time is to use a medical analogy. My feelings of inadequacy had turned into a *compound failure*. A compound *fracture* is when a bone is broken and it sticks out of the skin. A compound *failure* is when a person can no longer hide their brokenness because the failure has been exposed for the whole world to see. In this next illustration, embarrassment set in. I felt alone in my stupidity. Suffering from a *compound failure* can be devastating. My memory of this event is amazingly clear as it accurately reveals the desperation of my private need NOT to be a failure.

Desperate times calls for desperate measures

It was summer. Time to learn how to swim. My three siblings and I were all close enough in age that all four of us had been enrolled for those first sessions of lessons together.

Before we were allowed to actually get into the water we had to take the pre-beginners' class so we could go to that next level; the exciting part, getting into the water.

The sun was warm that summer morning as we

headed down to the modest beach our town generously provided. There were about ten children in our class, including the four of us.

We sat respectfully in a circle, around the instructor, in the warmth of the sand, roughly twenty feet from the water's edge.

She reviewed all of the water safety essentials, randomly asking us individually a few basic questions on what we had just learned. I was so excited! Soon would come the moment that we all waited for: Receiving those cute pre-beginner badges that would elevate us to that next level- getting into the water!

Finally, the time arrived for the presentation of honours...drum roll please! The instructor began calling the names of my fellow swimmers. One by one they went up to proudly accept the coveted certificate and badge of distinction. Everyone had been called forward and been given their pre-beginner badge except one person: Me! The teacher was now empty handed as she congratulated the others. The presentation was done.

I scrambled to my feet as I needed to *someway, somehow* let her know that *somewhere* a mistake had been made and I had been forgotten.

I stood spell-bound as the instructor motioned to all those who had now received their Pre-Beginners to move immediately to the edge of the water and get ready because, in just a few moments, they would start phase two in their new much-admired Beginners' class, and yes, that meant... getting into the water!

The young instructor now gently focused her gaze upon me, as if she was going to have to tell me that my dog just died. Tenderly she bent down and began to relay the disappointing news. She softly whispered, "Connie, you'll have to wait a little bit longer before you can get into the water. There's a few more safety rules you need to know."

With that said, she turned and started walking toward the others in the class who were waiting by the water's edge. The class was back in session with only one child absent: Me.

In disbelief, not knowing how to react, I slowly buried myself back into the comforting protective sand. Baffled by what had just occurred... a bit in a state of shock really... *What just happened?*

* * * *

By now you'd think this kind of experience would be familiar to me, almost a second nature. Call me naïve, but I have never anticipated these outcomes, nor did I ever get completely used to them.

I began drawing designs of nothing in particular in the sand, as my thoughts drifted to how I'd be able to fix this unfortunate setback. Periodically, I'd glance up to watch the class as they bobbed their heads in and out of the water. *The teacher must be right*, I thought to myself. *I wouldn't have been able to do that anyway.*

Then it dawned on me: The most brilliant idea anyone could have imagined and I had figured it out on my own! It occurred to me that the teacher had missed something so simple that even I understood. The answer was just under her nose and she hadn't even seen it. Miraculously, out of the clear blue, the answer to my problem had become clear to me.

I reeled with excitement as I asked myself some basic questions. *Did I really want to swim? Yes! Was my body capable of swimming if I knew how? BIG-yes! Weren't our bodies made to survive and adapt? DOUBLE-Yes!* These theories made SO much sense to me! How wonderful! Sink or swim. I knew I didn't want to sink, so that meant: *I will swim! I'm going to do this!*

In sheer delight, I clamoured to my feet, believing whole-heartedly that my idea was foolproof. Taking a moment to consider the area around me, I felt the need to get away from the class. They didn't need me as a distraction, anyway. Determined towards my new found mission, I needed to remain focused. I scooped up my towel and skipped towards the other end of the beach. Glancing around, not too far in the distance, I saw a dock projecting into the lake, secluded from the others on the beach.

In this particular spot, the water was deeper so that people could dive safely from the dock and not hit the bottom of the lake. I knew this. I also knew that I wouldn't be able to stand and touch the bottom of the lake at this spot. That worked perfectly into my plan.

In the past, whenever I tried to swim, I would inevitably touch one or both feet on the bottom of the lake. I believed that this was part of what prevented me from learning to swim. *In order for me to learn to swim I needed to not be able to touch the bottom*, thus taking my skills to the next level. With this in mind, I knew I needed to challenge myself to enter deeper water, creating a literal sink or swim scenario. This was my incredible brain wave that would solve the *me-not-swimming* problem… I was ready!

I glanced around and, to my amazement and pleasure; no one had noticed my movement up the beach. I walked to the end of the dock and stood peering into the water below. I was single-mindedly focused and positively resolved in my actions. *This was going to work!*

I considered once more how I needed to proceed. It dawned on me that in addition to not having the shallow water to fall back on, I'd also need to jump far enough away from the dock so that my instincts of grabbing the edge would not kick in and prevent me from swimming. *No time to waste! Sink or swim!* Taking a few necessary steps back to make a running jump off the dock... I was off...

...As I hit the water I was immediately overcome by the shock of going under. My thoughts instantly changed from, *man, what a great idea to holy crap, what have I done?* I thrashed about, struggling to bring my body to the surface. Submerged under the water, I was sinking (and yes, sinking was part of the equation, but in no way my preferred option!). I was now fighting for my life. Many thoughts raced through my head as I struggled to get my head above water. The harder I fought, the further away the surface seemed.

Oh dear God help me, I prayed. My thoughts whirled with concerns about my family and how they'd survive without me. *Would they be okay?*

The water was winning. I desperately needed to breathe. The struggle was intense. I thrashed as hard as I could but I was failing. My attempts to find the water's surface weren't working. Fighting for my life was horrendous. The sensation of drowning was unbearable. Wielding my last force of energy towards the surface... complete panic... Then, in an instant... it all changed.

Time slowed down to where it didn't seem to exist. Something altered during this silent moment that I cannot entirely explain. Stillness and peace surrounded me. I gazed upward towards the surface. My perspective from beneath the water fascinated me. Tranquillity soothed me as I sank deeper. It was weird and wonderful. I had no fear, no worries... *all was as it should be.*

Submerged in the murky water, I felt the most magnificent warmth, peace and acceptance imaginable. I was cradled by the stillness. I was no longer alone as a light illuminated me. The light knew me and loved me completely. I had an intense feeling of oneness with everything. The light revealed that we are all connected. It emanated pure love.

My visual perspective slowly transformed as I found myself gently floating over the water. I saw the dock and all the kids playing in and around the beach. I was at peace with my surroundings. Everything was beyond magnificent. So many thoughts and questions floated through my mind as all was revealed... *all was as it should be.*

I marvelled at the existence of everything below me and how miraculous it all truly was. Continuing to float even higher in the air, I viewed my little town and all of its splendour. Soon, I was floating even higher, above the clouds with an increasing sense of peace.

I became aware of the presence of another. A glowing figure floated beside me: A man dressed in white. He did not speak to me, yet communicated that everything was as it should be. I felt embraced by his light. Time no longer existed.

Suddenly, I found myself back in the water again. However, the feeling of serenity and peace continued to surround me. Looking up to the surface, I saw the luminous man reaching into the water towards me...*all was as it should be.*

The next thing I remember, I was curled up on my side, exhausted on the dock.

After some time, I lifted my head. I wanted to thank the man for saving me. However, there was no one there. It took me more than a few moments to pull myself together. Physically drained and emotionally confused, I didn't understand what had just happened. After much consideration, overwhelmed by everything, I decided to keep my near death experience to myself.

That evening, as my mother tucked me in to bed, she asked me why I was squishing myself against the wall on the far side of the bed, leaving more than half of my side of the bed unused. I grinned broadly and said, "I need to leave room for my angel!"

Years later, I shared with my family my memory of what I experienced that sunny summer day down by the beach. My mom's reaction was enlightening to me. She recalled, around that time, questioning if I might be suicidal due to my intense obsession with Heaven. My fascination with life after death had concerned my parents because I would often talk non-stop about Heaven and how wonderful it will be when we are done this part of our journey.

I am thankful for this experience. It has strengthened some of the beliefs I continue to hold dear. I believe something much more magnificent is waiting for us and because of this I believe we must live our life to its fullest.

Desperation + Irrational Action = More Desperation

My foolishness was not obvious to me due to my need to be *normal* and not fail once again. Although, I have to admit that in hindsight, I did see the foolishness of the idea instantly upon my immersion into the water.

In our lives, our plans don't always work out the way we envision them. Sometimes, when these moments of defeat occur, they can distort our view. We may feel that an immediate response is necessary to rectify the perceived problem.

Emotionally driven, we are less likely to think clearly, making the problem feel even more desperate than it actually is. Our emotions become entangled within our desperation, creating even more complications.

Desperation appears to be about mental and/or physical survival. The real question we should ask is: *Why do we feel desperate?* We all face challenges in life. The way in which we perceive a situation and how we confront these challenges, determines the effect that they have on us. When we react out of desperation, we (more often than not) make inappropriate choices… as I obviously had when attempting to swim.

Desperation can lead to negative consequences. When we are desperate, we often fail to analyze the conditions accurately. This means possibly drawing the wrong conclusions which may lead to wrong decisions. Wrong decisions lead to incorrect actions and incorrect actions create undesirable consequences.

Desperation, an aspect of fear, represents a legitimate physical and psychological response to difficult situations. We need to train ourselves to maintain a presence of mind during these times. Desperation makes us lose out and receive less than we deserve. We have more to gain when we do not act out of desperation.

When we are desperate for love, we may enter into relationships that are not good for us. When we are desperate for money, we may end up selling things for much less than they are worth. When we are desperate for acceptance, we may ignore our own needs. When we are desperate to seek refuge from an abusive relationship, we are more likely to jump right into another. When we are desperate not to feel internal or external pain, we may take drugs and substances to avoid our unacceptable reality.

When I allowed desperation to guide me, it impaired my judgment. Logic went straight out the window. This created within me an attitude where my actions could have easily cost me my life. On the flipside, we can use desperation to reveal what is not working and what we would like to change in our lives. Don't act out of desperation, use it as a guide. The quote below has a different and more positive angle on the subject:

"I don't think human beings learn anything without desperation. Desperation is a necessary ingredient to learning anything or creating anything. Period. If you ain't desperate at some point, you ain't interesting."

~ Jim Carrey

Veils of Pretense

All of us, without exception, have put on veils of pretence to survive moments in our lives. We do this to conceal our feelings of fear and inadequacy.

In no way should we feel badly for this response as it is part of our survival mechanism. It is when we stop knowing what is factual and lose sight of who we are that we do a major disservice to ourselves and to the people around us.

Having been raised in a strict fundamentalist Christian home, in the Bible belt, I found comfort attending services and youth events at one of the many local churches.

After about a year on my own I had begun to build a life outside of my former seclusion. During this time, I stumbled upon a handful of teenagers who welcomed me into their circle. Initially, I was reluctant to hang out with them. I had never developed friendships before. Until then my world had revolved around my many insecurities.

Like all teenagers this was a time of learning and development. We were innocent rebels hanging out till the breaking of dawn, talking about everything from life to death... and beyond.

Through these friends, I was introduced to a young man named Jeff. His popularity was obvious. He played in a band. All the girls wanted to date him. I, on the other hand, wasn't all that interested. He seemed nice enough, but he didn't seem to be my type, although, I had never dated. So, I didn't know my type.

Barely knowing this Jeff guy, on my eighteenth

birthday he presented me with a hand written card and a pack of gum (a sweet gesture). As a result of his kindness we started spending time together.

A few weeks into our budding friendship Jeff revealed his interest in wanting to date me. I wasn't interested and philosophized to him how "There are many fish in the sea" and that "I hadn't gotten my fishing license yet." To my amazement, this made him even more determined to spend time with me.

The only things we had in common were our lack of formal education and leaving home at an early age. However, Jeff's need to date me was stronger than my wavering self-love.

To make a long story short, the difference in time between when Jeff had given me that pack of gum until I was walking down the aisle, was less than five months.

I'm sure that my actions appeared to be utter insanity from an outside perspective, especially considering that I had tried three times, in vain, to break up with him during those months leading up to our wedding day.

I wanted what I wanted, but sadly, I didn't know what I wanted.

My parents were not in agreement with what I was about to do and refused to put their blessing upon the marriage. Consequently, this made it difficult for my siblings who didn't want to make waves in the family. I understood where everyone was coming from.

I felt no negative emotions towards any of my family for not coming to the wedding. I just wished they could support my decision.

I had asked Jeff if there was any way we could elope, instead of a formal wedding because of all of the uncomfortable controversy. He did not like that idea and his family would not have that for their son. Period.

Three weeks prior to the wedding, I had picked out my wedding dress with Jeff's mother. This was beyond difficult because I had always envisioned having my mother and my two sisters share these special moments with me.

I held back my feelings. I placed a smile on my face and endured what had become an emotionally painful experience.

We had been in the boutique for maybe five minutes when I found a dress in the discount section that caught my interest. It was nice enough and well below budget. It reminded me of the one my mother had worn on her wedding day. It had a form fitting bodice, becoming fuller as it draped gently down to the floor, just like my mom's dress had in the pictures of my parents wedding day.

I asked if I could try the dress on. After slipping into it I realized, to my disappointment, that the sleeves were too tight.

I poked my head out of the changing room and whispered "Do you have a size larger?" The lady, who was assisting me shook her head and said "I'm sorry; we don't have this particular style in another size."

With my growing need to be done the psychologically painful shopping I said, "Can you take the sleeves off and make it a sleeveless dress?"

The woman looked puzzled as she slowly answered "Yes. We can do that. But you haven't tried any other dresses on?"

"This dress is perfect" I whispered as I looked down at my feet. I quickly turned into the changing room as my tears streamed down my cheeks, betraying my cheerful persona.

* * * *

The morning of the wedding I was enveloped in my own fog, detached from what I was about to do. I forced myself to appear the happy bride, but truthfully, that was the last thing I was. I felt lost and alone.

My fiancé was busy getting ready, surrounded by family and friends. Having no one of my own to fill my time with, I decided to go for a walk to clear my head.

As I wandered around town thinking about how I would survive this day, I had a fantastic idea: *Maybe I should get my hair done for this occasion.*

Without delay, I continued walking, but now briskly to the closest hair salon. *I hope they have time?* I thought to myself.

Upon arrival I excitedly asked, "Do you have any openings today for a hair style?" The hairdresser looked at me shaking her head as she stated, "Saturdays are always very busy, we are completely booked up."

I nodded as I apologized, "I understand. I was just thinking how nice it would have been to get my hair done. I should have thought of it sooner. I'm getting married today." I thanked her and awkwardly turned toward the door.

The hairdresser's eyes widened as she responded "Wait. Wait, just a moment!" She immediately disappeared to the back room where the other hairdressers were working.

Moments later she returned and asked "What time is the wedding?"

I calmly told her, "Three in the afternoon." It was a little before noon at this time.

To this she replied with a big grin, "We'll take you right away!"

I was ecstatic. I couldn't believe they would rearrange their schedule for me. I felt humbled and grateful that they would go out of their way like that…for me.

After getting my hair styled, I felt one hundred times better. I continued walking over to Jeff's grandparents' house where my wedding gown had been delivered hours earlier. It was time to get this show on the road.

Upon arrival, I went straight to the room where my dress was waiting for me. As I slipped on the dress I was shocked by what I saw. *What on earth had they been thinking?*

It appeared the lady at the boutique had taken my words literally. Stunned, I stared at my reflection in the mirror. The sleeves appeared to have been brutally ripped off. The dress looked unfinished and utterly ridiculous. The boutique hadn't even bothered to sew down the edges of where the sleeves had once been.

"Oh no!"

My inability to endure the emotionally painful dress shopping had created a dreadful outcome. Heartbroken, I was at a loss as to what to do. If I would have just looked at the dress sooner I might have anticipated this predicament and maybe, I would have been able to rectify it.

The house was a bustle of activity. Everyone was busy in the kitchen preparing the food that was going to be served at the reception.

Jeff's grandma must have sensed something was wrong. "Is there anything I can do for you?" she lovingly asked.

I looked down at the floor and whispered "The dress

needs help."

    I knew I didn't have time to fix it. I had to finish getting ready. I grabbed one of the threads that were dangling where the sleeves had once been "If I would have known this sooner I could have sewn on some lace on these open seams, which would have been at least a bit better."

    Grandma nodded in agreement as she slowly walked to the corner of the room and opened up a drawer. She took out a needle and thread, and then, with a bit of white lace that she magically had in her collection of material, she tacked the lace in place, making the sleeves appear finished.

    She did all this while I was still wearing the dress. I felt like Cinderella as I gave her an enormous hug. "Thank you, thank you!" I said as I hurried off to the other room to finish getting ready…

This was my sad reality. I was in this situation because I didn't know how to speak up for myself. My need to have everyone like and accept me overruled my own desires for happiness. I had given up my will.

    You see, a few days prior to our wedding day, I had worked up enough nerve to have another heart-to-heart with my fiancé and let him know my Truth. I had tried, or at least I had thought I had tried to break up with Jeff a few times before, but had been unsuccessful. Maybe, I hadn't been clear enough.

    It took everything in me to do what seemed to be the impossible. Apologetically, I told Jeff that I didn't believe I loved him the way I should; the way he deserved. His reaction was not at all as I had anticipated. He smiled as if he knew. He responded by saying "That's okay. I have enough love for the both of us." He elaborated, stating that if he didn't love me as much as he did, he would have never put up with me attempting to break up with him as often as I had tried.

His point made sense to me at the time. I saw how very sad it made him over the thought of losing me. I felt extremely selfish to have even thought of bringing up my hesitation and subjecting him to my desires once again.

Having unsuccessfully revealed my Truth, I continued to shove my feelings deeper within me. Dejected... I thanked him for his understanding, for loving me so much to NOT let me go.

At this particular time in my life, my need to be transparent had become all-consuming. My inner turmoil had forced me to reveal the uncertainty I felt. Unfortunately, even with my resolve that the relationship was not right for me, I hadn't succeeded in saving myself from what I didn't want. I had failed! The question then is, *why?* In hindsight, my inability to assert my desires stood no chance because I didn't believe that I was worth it, that I mattered enough to fight for what I wanted.

Yes it's true; I went through the motions of defending my inner dreams of freedom. The problem was that I had no base of self-love to fall back on, making the attempt to change my destiny futile before I even began.

So, when I did finally build up enough courage to say what I felt and the response wasn't perfect, I backed away from my Truth. Yes... I could state it until the cows come home; I fought the good fight and lost. I could even say that I told him so, but that isn't entirely true. I didn't stand up for my thoughts or my sincere feelings. I turned my back on myself when I allowed his thoughts and his feelings to be more important than my own.

Inadvertently, I reinforced my personal belief that my feelings didn't matter when I accepted his rejection of my desires. I was doing myself a great disservice. In saying all this, I am not defending his enforcement to control, but I was allowing it by not reaffirming my Truth.

Before we start any meaningful relationship, we need to learn to love ourselves. Until we can do this, we aren't able to love anyone else. It may be cliché, but if we want real love, then we need to have enough self-confidence and self-respect to unconditionally accept ourselves for who we are. Then in turn, we can accept others as they are.

This doesn't mean that we have to be conceited. We just need to respect and trust ourselves as we humbly accept our flaws. A side benefit to this is that we will be more relaxed and comfortable around other people and, as such, more likely to attract people who also love themselves, making for much healthier relationships. This also includes our friendships.

"Unless your heart, your soul, and your whole being are behind every decision you make, the words from your mouth will be empty, and each action will be meaningless. Truth and confidence are the roots of happiness."

~ Kathleen Pederson

Bubble of Denial

Having completed that difficult walk down the aisle, through the overcrowded room, I faced my soon-to-be husband. He finished his song and put down his guitar. An awkward silence filled the room. The tension in the air was agonizing.

If only this day could be over, I thought to myself.

He took his place beside me at the base of the stage. The best man and the bridesmaid stood next to us. I had just asked my bridesmaid days earlier to take the place of my sister Jacquie due to the conflict with my family regarding this wedding.

We had invited approximately 80 people to the wedding, however, over 150 people showed up. The small building was overflowing beyond capacity with friends, family and a handful of complete strangers looking for some interesting gossip.

The town had been buzzing with rumours for weeks due to the secrecy that shrouded the details of this day. *Why? Is she pregnant? What's the rush? Why are her parents not involved? How come they have a guard at the door? Why have this wedding in this tiny little building??? Why? Why? Why?*

There was only one pastor we could convince to marry us and he was standing before us on the modest stage. His voice was flat and lifeless as he mumbled the necessary lecture of our vows.

Halfway through the ceremony a soft thud was heard over the murmur of the preacher. The room gasped. The best man had blacked out and had fallen into the audience and was now lying on my grandmother's lap. Glancing back at this scene, I giggled to myself. I found it a refreshing break from the soberness of the moment. The heat of too many bodies in such a small space had been overwhelming to him. After a moment he was able to compose himself and we resumed the service.

Soon after, I was being asked if I would take the man beside me to be my lawfully wedded husband. My mouth took over before my mind engaged as I stated, "I do!" outwardly without my inward permission... and...the deed was done!

I experienced many firsts that evening. The first time I ever got drunk. The first time I threw up because of being drunk. The first time (and last) time I threw up *on* my husband. The first time I enjoyed a cool porcelain toilet against my face... and the first night I ever slept on a cold bathroom floor... What a day!!

What a ridiculous, unbelievable, perfect example of what fear of disapproval can do to our thoughts and the disturbing decisions we may make due to such fears.

Hindsight being 20/20, it's easy to see the insanity of my actions. At the time however, it was merely a matter of survival. Because I couldn't stand up for myself, it was easy for someone else to guide me away from my feelings. Even though it was not what I would have wished, I had bought into it.

How sad is that?

Losing sight of who we are in order to feel accepted is a sad reality of too many people. When we continually put other people's wants and needs above our own, we damage the core of who we are. We may also be hurting the people that we think that we are helping.

I know of no other creature that would go against instinct, judgment and common sense just because something (or someone) talked it out of its opinion. Funny how we humans can be so unaware!

How we react to our circumstances will depend on whether or not we are seeking acceptance from others. Our need for acceptance creates within us the illusion that we don't matter; that we are not worthy of our own needs and desires. We give up our individuality when we do not acknowledge our personal needs. When we choose to blend in, deciding not to disappoint the people around us, we lose ourselves to the big picture.

Many of us have a difficult time being honest with ourselves. I have learned this because I am among the many. Remaining true to ourselves; the core of who we are, can be one of the largest struggles we'll deal with throughout our lives. People pleasers, in particular, will have to pay special attention to this constant challenge.

We cannot be truthful with others if we are not aware of our own Truth. Unless you break free from this need to be accepted at any cost, you will never be capable of being entirely honest with others.

Many of us have a hard time recognizing our personal Truth due to numerous factors, including our upbringing and beliefs. Some of us have even gone so far as to give up the majority of our personal control so that we could be in the life of another, doing this at the high cost of losing who we are in the process.

Allowing someone else to define who we are causes us to lose our ability to discover and continue to grow as an individual. We lose the capacity to discern our Truth from their Truth; real from false. For countless numbers of us who have accepted the illusion that we don't matter, the road to discovering what is true *(our Truth)* will take focused energy and determination.

Waving a magic wand would be the most magnificent and effortless way to rectify this kind of brain programming. Alas, I have not been able to locate this miraculous utensil, so I encourage you to read on.

Accepting ourselves can be difficult, but with time, patience, and self-love, we can do it. When we permit our genuine self to surface and become authentic with those who share our world, we are giving our gift of self. This might initially appear impossible. However, as we work through our insecurities, we build strength and healthy boundaries.

I know how difficult the journey to self-discovery is. I also know how satisfying it is when I have allowed my voice to come forth. The joy and freedom I feel when the real *me* is exposed is an indescribable, liberating experience. I strongly suggest the path of Truth. The journey is worth it!

Truth is rooted in love. The greatest act of love that you can give to yourself and anyone else is living a life of transparency. If you are willing to be transparent, you will respect yourself and, in turn, others will respect you too.

> *"This above all; to thine own self be true and it must follow, as the night the day, Thou cannot then be false to any man."*
>
> ~ *William Shakespeare*

Authenticity

For those of us who find it difficult to love ourselves, being authentic is difficult, but attainable. When we look within for our self-worth, we no longer need the approval of others. This gives us the freedom to be individuals, acceptable in our own eyes, the ones that matter most.

The proverb *"The Truth shall set you free"* is the key to healing and growing into a strong, independent person, even with the risk of negative reactions from others. When we allow our self to surface, we bring light into the darkness of our unknowing. When we walk in our Truth, we walk in light, and when we walk in our light we live a more purposeful, fulfilled life.

Having different wants and needs than someone else is natural. However, to disregard these differences are not! People who have ever had to hide who they were, for whatever reason, will tell you they were miserable in their inability to release their Truth. Find your Truth and live it! If you don't, it's not much of a life at all. Besides, who wants to walk around pretending to be someone else when the best character is the genuine person within?

You are the best person for the job of being *you*. If you are ever going to tap into your greatest potential, you need to be honest with yourself, so you can release yourself (the authentic self) to the waiting world. You fail yourself the most when you deny your very essence: The real you!

Experts in the science of human character have observed that individuals who are not living authentically often lose their meaning, purpose, and drive for life and become more susceptible to chronic anxiety, boredom, and fatigue that often lead to depression. These individuals also have a tendency to pursue quick-fixes such as sedating themselves with alcohol or drugs, or living in fantasies to avoid experiencing life.

I know this because I did this in a variety of forms (food being my primary drug of choice), largely because I was not in touch with the harmony which comes from living my Truth. I was completely oblivious to the root of my discontent.

The Day the Bubble Burst

My sadness grew as I began to comprehend the significance of my decision to fuse myself to dysfunction. For reasons unknown to me, my actions hadn't repaired anything, they had only made matters worse. The first time I experienced his physical rage was the day after our wedding.

After only a few months of marriage we packed up our things and moved away. We had been given the opportunity to manage a restaurant in a small town about two and a half hours west of our familiar home of Altona.

It was a fresh start in Killarney, Manitoba. Maybe my insecure husband wouldn't feel judged anymore. Maybe he'd be able to control his temper. I felt helpless to stop his fits of anger. I craved for normalcy. *Who knows? Maybe this move might just be the miracle I'd been praying for.*

Due to my low self-esteem, I felt deserving of the

abuse. I believed deep within me that the punishments I received must somehow suit the crime.

When provoked to the point where he could no longer control his anger, he lashed out at me. Powerless in the face of his outbursts, I thought that if I could just make life easier for him he wouldn't experience these uncontrollable emotions. I felt personally responsible for his anger, reaffirming my shame. My humiliation grew as his emotional instability continued to deteriorate my self-worth.

The weirdest part was that I felt unworthy of his regretful apologies. I'd think to myself, *no one would deliberately act out such uncontrolled anger unless it was warranted.* This created even more guilt in me, adding to my already low self-confidence. My brain processed the abuse much easier than his tearful apologies which predictably followed the outbursts. Deep within me, I felt deserving and so the cycle continued...

    Nineteen now and settling into our new life together. The façade of happiness wasn't hard to maintain. You see, I'd worn the mask of survival most of my life. Denying the source of fresh bruises was also surprisingly easy. As soon as they surfaced, revealing the ugly truth, I'd think up different ways I could have received them in case anyone asked.

    Nearly believing my own lies allowed me to repeat my prepared stories of clumsiness when deemed necessary. I also learned to value long sleeves that could be worn year round, so as not to have to explain the unexplainable.

    I'd made my choice to marry and believed that there was no turning back. I was stuck, unless I'd be willing to admit that I'd made a mistake. Too proud to seek help, I only revealed to my family and the community a reflection of happiness.

In our new location I stumbled upon my great distraction: Unlimited access to greasy fried food from the restaurant my husband managed. This instantly satisfied my inner worthlessness. However, the feeling of contentment didn't last. Before long, it was time to fill the emptiness again. I filled myself with food and felt better. When the numbness started wearing off, I ate some more. This made life easier because I didn't want to feel. I didn't know how to deal with my pain. Coping wasn't necessary when food could fill that void.

I avoided mirrors. They didn't make me feel good. I even went so far as to avoid glancing into shopping store windows fearing that I might catch a glimpse of my expanding reflection. That reality did not fit into this bubble of denial which I was content to be trapped in.

About a year into this whirlwind of food-addiction, almost sixty pounds heavier, it happened. It was around two in the morning following a previous evening stupor of creamy whipped desserts that I awoke to a sharp stabbing pain pulsating through my stomach. I gasped for some crucial air. Nauseated, my eyes blurred from the intense pain.

"Oh my, Oooooh God?!"

My body twisted in agony; I bent over and shuffled to the bathroom and immediately started to throw up. Reeling in pain, I couldn't decide which part of me needed the toilet more as my insides were exploding from both ends. I called to my husband to get me a pail as I sat drained and limp on the toilet. The room was spinning. I desperately tried to gain my equilibrium.

What's happening to me?

My thoughts swirled as I slipped into nothingness, hitting my head on the side of the bathtub, and falling into a heap upon the floor. It was evident that I needed a hospital.

My husband, who had never handled emergencies well, started screaming about needing to take me to the hospital. Drenched in sweat from the shock of my nightmarish ordeal, I agreed.

Taking short deliberate breaths, I gasped, "Give me a moment to get ready, and we'll go."

In his need to control an uncontrollable condition, Jeff started tugging me out of the bathroom as I fought desperately, holding onto the doorway wanting...no...needing to first get dressed. I was in complete agony, but pleaded to retain my dignity. The tug of war was worth it. His frustration over my stubbornness gave way to his anger as he released me, allowing me to cover up my nakedness.

About two hours after being admitted to the hospital all the symptoms disappeared and I fell into an exhausted sleep.

Extensive medical probing and tedious testing revealed I had developed gallstones. What I'd experienced had *just* been a gallbladder attack. When I say *just* I am using the light and airy way it was revealed to me...and to me it was NOT just a *just!*

My point: When we hide from our feelings, we create a bubble of denial around us which WILL inevitably burst.

My method of coping betrayed me. In addition to my

underlying issues that were not being dealt with, my new physical ailment could not be ignored. I was in the habit of running from my emotions. I had to search for new methods of avoidance... so I could continue to deceive myself.

I needed a new escape.

During this time, I didn't know that I was running from myself, avoiding my unacceptable circumstances. I was desperate to continue my subconscious survival tactics while remaining in my familiar surroundings of contradiction. Unaware of my deeper issues, I remained focused on the surface, oblivious to the core of my problem.

I have changed and altered my obsessions and distractions throughout my life. Ultimately I have found that the only cure for this affliction of denial is living an authentic life.

By the way, being authentic does not mean being perfect. It just means doing your best through truth and humility. Sometimes that means exposing your warts and blemishes, since the true beauty of authenticity lies within imperfection.

It was not fear that held me back from my reality; it was the absence of me, not acknowledging my existence. I didn't know it, but I was running from myself.

> *"We can ignore reality, but we cannot ignore the consequences of ignoring reality."*
>
> *~ Ayn Rand*

Core Values

If you want to grow as a person, it is imperative you face the fears that make you turn against your values: Your core. Your values are the things that you believe are important. When the things that you do and the way that you behave match your values, life feels right. When these don't align with your values, things feel wrong and can be a real source of discontentment.

The best way to identify your core values is to be aware of what is steering your choices, so you don't just coast on autopilot. Yes, operating on autopilot is the easiest way to glide through life because you don't have to think. You just sit back and let life take you in the direction it's headed. But be forewarned, if that's the choice you make, your life will never be your own. You are relinquishing control, allowing the world, the wind, and other people to direct your destiny.

An airplane is a great illustration of the need for integrity. It is essential that the plane's integrity is at its finest before it takes to the air. When we are confident in the stability of the plane, we know that when it encounters turbulence, it will handle it.

When we live with integrity, we reflect outwardly our inner character. We act from motives, interests, and values that are completely our own. Everyone has values, attitudes, and beliefs, even if they don't know it. When we live an authentic life, we live a life that resonates with full meaning... *our* meaning.

Integrity * √ (Value$_1$)(Value$_2$)(Value$_n$) = Behaviour

Integrity rooted in our Core Values reveals our Behavior

Understanding your motivation for why you do what you do comes from understanding yourself. What exactly do you stand for? What values are important? Taking the time to define your values gives you the opportunity to question them. Are they working for you or against you? Are they your own values or those imposed upon you?

With awareness comes knowledge, with knowledge comes Truth, and with Truth comes the opportunity for change. You cannot change things that you are not aware of. As a result of being open to yourself, you give yourself the opportunity to transform for the better. Actions reveal inner beliefs and values. You are guiding your life by what you value.

A person's integrity is like the foundation of a building. We would not build the same foundation for a shed as we would for a high-rise since a foundation needs to be capable of supporting the weight of whatever will be placed upon it. The consequences of switching foundations could be catastrophic; perhaps not for a light shed, but certainly for a heavier building. Our personal foundation must be solidly built and capable of supporting us through the darkest and toughest of times.

Without a strong personal foundation, you won't have the stability to carry you through the inevitable tough times ahead. As a result, you'll continually be building temporary shelters just to get you through one crisis after another.

Without permanent values in place, this process will have to be repeated frequently.

Your character is what keeps you strong when you encounter unforeseen dilemmas and transitions. Your strength of character becomes most evident when faced with both emotional and physical hardships. Spending time building a strong character is important to your future stability.

With your character strengthened, you'll move forward with more confidence and assurance. Knowing that you have a strong foundation, which is based on your own personal integrity, reinforces your stability.

People with integrity have strong ethics. One of the most significant things we can do for ourselves is to work on our character. The best way to do this is by becoming aware of what we stand for. Being an honest and reliable person is a wonderful start.

People with integrity realize that everything they do is a statement of who they are. Your integrity is demonstrated in your willingness to stick to the values that are important to you. It's easy to make promises but often difficult to keep them. Every time you keep a promise, it's an act of integrity which, consequently, strengthens the quality of your character.

"Integrity is doing what you say you'll do, and saying what you truly think, even if unpopular."

~ Unknown

So, how do you develop positive characteristics? Aspire to be consistent, remain honest with yourself and others. Strive for a flawless nature, bearing in mind, it is impossible to be flawless or perfect. Shooting for this goal will move you closer toward it, improving and strengthening your integrity.

Value vs. Volume
Substance vs. Style
Sharing vs. Selfish
Grateful vs. Griping
Honesty vs. Hypocrisy
Joyous vs. Jealous
Conversation vs. Conflict
Forgiveness vs. Fighting
Integrity vs. Instability
Love vs. Loathing
Purpose vs. Passive
Transparency vs. Trickery
Virtue vs. Vengeful

You cannot be perfect and you never will be. When you inevitably fall short of perfection; give yourself the grace to fail as you continue to make mistakes. Part of the process of moving forward is failing. You will always fail in trying to achieve perfection because perfection is not attainable. Remain steadfast in striving for your best as you continue moving forward in your quest to evolve into a better individual.

Be kind to yourself when you fail. If your standards were lower, you would not fail as often. When you unreasonably raise the standard of what you expect from yourself, you will fail more.

To attain your own high standards live your personal beliefs. Your beliefs will then be reflected through your actions, actions you can be proud and pleased to be a part of. These are the actions that will help transform your inner world and therefore help transform your outer world.

"You can search throughout the entire universe for someone who is more deserving of your love and affection than you are yourself, and that person is not to be found anywhere. You yourself, as much as anybody in the entire universe deserve your love and affection."

~ Buddha

Transparency

Life has a strange way of exposing us. Even as I write this, the realization that there is so much left to learn is overwhelming, yet liberating. Believe it or not, there is freedom in admitting one's ignorance; letting go of the need to be perfect. Trying to keep up with our false perceptions is draining and self-defeating.

This next story I will share is a great example of what appeared to be *the perfect family*. I wish I had not set up the illusion of the perfect me, the perfect family, and the perfect life.

There is a ripple effect to all we do. Even if we think we are covering up for the good of all, we tend to do more damage to those we love, and to ourselves, without anticipating the impact of our actions.

Abuse is not acceptable in any form and we should never stand for it. We need to seek to free ourselves and others from the control it has. The only way we can do this is by shining a light on this intolerable epidemic. If we can become collectively strong, we can move through our shame, no longer covering it up and allowing it to continue: Stepping out of the shadows to move forward. With this open approach, even the abusers can come clean from the turmoil they, too, experience. Consequently, those experiencing the volatility of domestic violence will no longer feel the need to hide in shame and embarrassment, but rather deal with their individual issues and move forward.

Important note: I do not want to come across as a victim. For years I enabled what took place behind closed doors. In fact, without realizing it, my personal identity had been built around my inner turmoil and sadness. I embraced my misery as some sort of Medal of Honour I had earned. Maybe I did this to justify what I did not understand. Maybe by doing this, I felt deserving of the personal excuses it afforded me. I don't fully know.

The Million Dollar Family

We lived in a beautiful, well kept, three bedroom home, peacefully situated in our quiet rural town. We were back in Altona where we had originally met and married sixteen years earlier. We had moved back years earlier to be close to all of our family.

Jeff and I had been blessed with two wonderful children, a girl and a boy. Our daughter Amber was nine and our son, Michael, had just turned eight. The school playground behind our house doubled as our extended back yard. Life looked picture perfect.

My husband and I had become very involved in the community. Raising two children in the Bible belt, a tightly knit religious town, appeared to be what dreams are made of.

Behind the façade of perfection, my heart yearned for Truth. On the other hand, I loved the role of being a Mom and embraced every facet of it. Cooking, baking, sewing costumes for dress up, painting bedrooms for childhood fantasies, I loved it all! The hustle and bustle of life distracted me from the secrets lurking behind closed doors.

Things had calmed down somewhat as our marriage evolved. Jeff didn't fly into a rage as often as he once did; his behaviour had altered so as not to be as transparent to our children and the watching world.

I continued to be an enabler by hiding my feelings in order to keep his anger subdued. I would take responsibility for his uncontrolled outbursts. This ultimately created further pain and anguish within me. This need I had to protect him from himself was destroying me.

One day after one of his heated episodes, I'd gone walking with a friend who happened to be a counsellor from our church. Yes, I had a new bruise, but I hadn't even considered disclosing the manner in which it had been received.

Soon after coming home from my walk, Jeff flew off the handle as he angrily accused me of *"ratting him out."* I was confused. I didn't know what he was talking about. Without any further discussion, he blasted out the door, headed straight to the church to extinguish the *"unsubstantiated rumours."*

As he stormed into the pastor's office, he proclaimed defiantly, "Yes! I do hit her… sometimes, but nothing like I used to!"

The pastor was dumbfounded, as he had not heard of any abuse allegations before this. He immediately requested to see me.

Within the hour, I anxiously paced back and forth in the hallway of the church, waiting to be summoned into the office. I was scared. I didn't know what I was going to say.

The pastor opened the door and motioned for me to enter. No sooner had I sat down in front of his desk and the pastor began questioning me, "What's happening?"

I softly responded, "It's true."

Disconnected from my feelings, I stared numbly at

my feet. The emotions that should have poured from me were nonexistent. I'd lived with this secret for so long; I didn't know how to react.

My mind drifted back to the words, I had just uttered. I became aware of my opportunity for escape; the freedom of Truth had suddenly made things transparent. I recognized my prison doors had swung open.

I slowly looked up to the pastor and whispered "I can't do this anymore, I'm done!"

In this particular moment, even though I felt free from a facade, I also felt like the biggest failure ever. I felt that the whole town needed the illusion to continue. My husband was the head of a charity youth drop-in centre in town and because of his position he was highly respected by the religious community. Now, because of my inability to hide the truth, his job would be in jeopardy.

I was also involved in a separate youth program through the church. I felt sad for everyone who would be affected by this news. I knew I'd also be letting the young people down who looked up to us. Without a doubt, the most innocent victims through all of this would be my children, undeserving of the aftermath of what transpired through the division and destruction of their world: The break-up of their family. The personal turmoil they would have to endure because I was no longer able to keep up the appearance of *the perfect family* weighed heavily upon me.

Wearing a mask of approval; pretending to be something or someone we're not is a great description of living a smothered existence: A private hell. When we do this, we validate our shame because we feel unworthy. This reinforces our lack of self-worth, verifying what we fear: We have no real value. This is a lie many people buy into. A lie strengthened by hiding. We believe that we are inferior even though there is no basis of truth to this lie.

The real you who lies dormant behind a facade cannot be revealed through pretence. It is impossible to communicate Truth when you are unaware of your own Truth. Transparency in your life is imperative for acceptance and healing. As you recognize and acknowledge your weaknesses, your strengths can be developed.

Freedom from any self-imposed prison is obtained through awareness. The wisdom you gain from personal awareness will provide you with the keys to change the things that you'd like to change, to create the life of your own choosing. Without awareness of the core of who you are, self-acceptance and change become impossible.

Transparency creates clarity. Clarity empowers.

As you become aware of why you do what you do and feel what you feel you can make changes. Once you recognize your significance, you will no longer allow anyone (including yourself) to hide who you are. Please love yourself enough to make the extra effort to appreciate your unique greatness.

Shining the light of Truth within the darkness disintegrates the lies that keep you trapped. You no longer need to maintain your agonizing secrecy.

After sixteen years of marriage, it was over. The day of the aftermath, I sat down and emotionally wrote this poem;

In the midst of my heartache,
All is well

I am enveloped in a storm raging 'round about me,
I should be swept away by the whirlwinds of sadness,
Yet, here I stand!

The cold, bitter bite of self-hatred,
Long would have been my demise,
Yet, here I stand!

The deafening thunder bolts of abuse,
Not knowing when they would strike,
Should have brought me to my knees,
Yet, here I stand!

The torrential demoralizing words pelting down on me,
Burning deeper than any lightning bolt could,
Yet, here I stand!

The storm is not within me anymore.
I am not the weak vessel perceived by the storm.

I realize now,
I am standing!

My prayer:
Someday, I may learn to walk.

Excommunicated

Through the process of writing this book, I have been forced to confront some of the unresolved issues involving different forms of rejection and abuse that I have experienced in my life.

When struggling with difficulties, we tend to lean on family and friends for advice and validation. If we are fortunate, we have such people around us: Our parents, a partner, siblings co-workers, and friends. We all have the need for love and acceptance.

It's comforting and essential to have these connections. It's also nice if we have a community that provides a place of security, guidance and support. A church can be a great place for this, however, like anything that we become dependent on, it can be taken away.

As individuals it is natural to want to hide the things that we feel shame and embarrassment over. An organization is no different. In order to understand the people who uphold the rules within such an organization, we need to understand why the people within the church do what they do.

The church only has the authority to discipline within the church body. The leadership is responsible to shepherd those who have agreed to follow the rules and laws of the church, through membership. The main objective of the following ritual was to seek the atonement of two believers who had fallen into sin, commonly known as *church discipline*.

Being active members of this Mennonite Church, Jeff and I were required to go before the leadership to address their concerns regarding our marital breakdown and our uncertain future within the organization.

As I sat waiting for the meeting to begin, the room was silent. The lyrics from an old hymn played through my thoughts; *my eyes are dry, my faith is old, my heart is hard, my prayers are cold.* The words in the song reinforced my crushing guilt. I hung my head in shame.

The pastor began with a prayer for guidance. The sound of Jeff's sobbing created a disturbing backdrop to the surreal experience.

I had no words to defend my broken spirit. After a long drawn out pause, one of the deacons asked me, "Is there any way you can stay in the marriage?" I looked down and softly relied, "Yes, but, I will die. I don't mean Jeff will kill me. I mean, my heart, my soul will die." The room fell completely silent.

My eyes stayed focused on the floor as my mind wandered, *I wish I could cry as Jeff could. If I was connected to my feelings they would be able to see how broken I am. I seem to have separated myself from myself. Maybe I've been playing a role for so long that I can no longer recognize my true feelings? It's probably good that I can't cry; if I truly felt this pain, I might not be able to stop.*

After what seemed to be a lifetime of silence, they reluctantly agreed that a temporary separation would be granted.

I didn't know it at the time, but I was guided by fear and controlled by guilt. I was afraid to let others know about my sins, temptations, struggles, and doubts. Because this had become my learned response, I was oblivious to my own emotions. I revealed only what I thought was acceptable.

Conformity had become my survival tool. I had grown into a perfectionist, idealistic young mother and wife. I worked diligently to prove to the people within the church through service, how important I was. Maybe they would accept me, and, through their acceptance, I could learn to accept myself.

We are all afraid of something. One of my greatest fears was that people wouldn't accept me. After joining the church, I became involved in the youth program. I volunteered to clean the church every week. I shoveled the snow and kept the sidewalks looking their best. I set up chairs for conferences and cleaned up after them. I loved helping because it confirmed my role within the church.

    Because Jeff appeared genuinely remorseful for his *sins* he was forgiven by the church leadership, maintaining his membership within the church.
    I, on the other hand, was not willing to continue the cycle of abuse. His tearful apology was not new to me. I had become numb to what I had grown to see as emotional manipulation. I'm not saying that he wasn't sorry; I believe he was, however, I had suffered through his hot and cold temperament long enough - I was done.
    The church sanctioned the separation, tolerated only due to the extreme circumstances within the marriage. However, when I filed for divorce after a year of the separation, it created a whole different upheaval and because of this I received a letter from the Pastor and was formally

excommunicated from the Mennonite Brethren Church.

The more extreme discipline for disobedience within the church is placing the sinner outside the communion of fellowship. This is called excommunication. After I was publicly disciplined by the church the people within our religious community had no choice but to turn their back on me as well. The word that traditionally describes this action is "shunning."

Guilt makes us believe that we have done something wrong; shame makes us believe *we* are bad. Shame is humiliation, because shame, in its most extreme experience, conveys that one is not fit to live in one's own community. Shame is the inner experience of feeling worthless, rejected, and cast-out.

I felt lost in a world that I thought had no spiritual meaning. Thankfully, I learned in the months ahead how ignorant I had been in my Christian snobbery. It was in the weakening of my identity that I eventual saw how opinionated and judgemental I had been concerning others and myself.

Shame is so painful, so debilitating that people who suffer from it often develop numbing and destructive coping strategies to avoid its tortures of self-hatred. When the Truth is fully recognized, survivors can begin their recovery. But far too often, secrecy prevails and the traumatic event surfaces as a physical symptom.

"Never feel shame for trying and failing for he who has never failed is he who has never tried."

~ Og Mandino

Reality Check

Who is the best person to ask about you? You are! Who feels the emotions that are buried within you? You do! Who knows more about your inner world than you? Nobody! No one knows more about you than you!

If you fully understood this, you would stop asking others about who you are and start asking the person who knows: You! Deep down, you know so much more than you give yourself credit for. What are you afraid of?

It seems people who cannot deal with reality run from it. The way we do this varies depending on our coping skills.

Running from our feelings is self-defeating. How can we make rational decisions and choices if we do not face reality?

If you want to take ownership of your life, it is important to understand why you do what you do. Is it possible that you are running or hiding from a reality that seems too difficult to face?

Take off your blindfold so that you can take control of your destiny. Taking ownership of your actions allows you to face your fears. If you insist on running around blindfolded, you will likely run into a wall... as I did.

The day the Running Stopped

Breaking news: In disbelief, I watched as the cameras captured the horrific scenes as they unfolded. The date was September 11th and the World Trade Centre had just been hit.

We all have our own detailed memory of where we were and what we were doing the tragic day that the Trade Centre was destroyed. A moment that will remain etched in our minds forever.

As I watched the tragedy which was unfolding, my thoughts moved to all of the untold victims. The need for blood donations would be immense with a disaster this huge.

I was sadly aware I was not one who could spare that precious gift. I'd been bleeding for weeks and my condition was getting progressively worse.

I rationalized my denial; I didn't have time for the inconvenience of the bleeding. I needed to maintain the appearance of normalcy at all costs. My children depended on me to keep things as consistent as possible; money had to be made, bills needed to be paid.

On top of all that, if this situation didn't fix itself, I'd have to deal with the embarrassment; The embarrassment that would have to be endured by having to expose my failing body; admitting to my doctor that I was and had been bleeding for some time from my lower intestines. That thought didn't please me. My need to run from the Truth over-shadowed any rational thinking.

Barely able to tear myself from the live news broadcast of those terrible events, I had to get to work; my clients would soon be waiting. I gathered up my things, left the apartment, and walked across the street to the hospital where I had a few months earlier moved my business.

The decision to move had been a tough one. Emerson was a non-religious town about a 20 minute drive east of Altona. My choice to separate us from the community had been made easier after I received the *'excommunication letter'* from the church.

While Jeff and I were still married, I operated my physiotherapy business from my home, but after divorce and the division of assets, that was no longer feasible. The house had to be sold.

    For my therapy business I rented a room in the Emerson hospital, conveniently adjacent to the waiting room. It was a tiny room; scarcely large enough to fit my massage bed; just enough room for me to move around in, but I loved it! Enjoying all the staff who drifted around the hospital was a real treat compared to the solitude of working from my home.
    Having full custody of both Amber and Michael, affordability dictated we scrimp and save. I rented a small 520 square foot, one bedroom basement apartment in our new town of Emerson. We would improvise until my finances stabilized.
    Our living space turned out to be a bit of a challenge. The apartment had a storage room that now doubled as a second bedroom for my daughter and son. Needless to say Amber and Michael were not thrilled at the concept of having to share a tiny bedroom. Powerless to play any role in the decisions, they endured the life altering transition and appeared to handle the inconvenience considerably well.
    In order to utilize the small living space, I had put most of our belongings in storage behind my dad's store in

Altona. I traded some of the furniture that we didn't need for the bunk beds the kids would have to tolerate until our lives would settle. This aided in creating our little nest of transition.

When Amber or Michael would complain of our undersized surroundings, I encouraged them to view the experience as an adventure. When deemed necessary, I would share stories from my childhood winter in a garage. "You guys are so lucky. When I was your age I had to live in a garage, with my brothers, sister and a pregnant mom and dad without the luxury of an indoor bathroom!" That statement always had them rolling their eyes... bringing an end to their grumbling... for that moment.

To make the transition less disruptive, my daughter and son would need to take a bus in order to remain in their old school. Just shy of an hour bus ride, morning and afternoon, would have to be tolerated every day. After considering the options, this was the best solution.

Amber and Michael had already taken the bus to school that morning and my work day had begun.

Concealing from my world the severity of my condition, I moved forward with my day's activities. My lack of sufficient life-giving blood depleted my energy levels significantly. This day seemed tougher than the ones before.

My strategic use of coffee that normally gave me that artificial energy was not doing its job.

* * * *

Soon after I set up my business in the Emerson hospital, I became friends with many of doctors and staff. When the doctors and I would go out for lunch, they would often comment on my excessive coffee intake. Dr. Munsamy had light-heartedly threatened an intervention one week earlier. Truth was, excessive coffee had become necessary for my survival, but now it was not doing the job.

My ritual was to wander into the lab to visit with Leona, one of the lad techs, prior to starting my work day. We'd catch up on all our latest escapades, however, today was different. Today's conversation was filled with the serious updates involving the Trade Centre in New York.

As we talked, I casually asked, "Do you think you would be able to check my blood level? I want to see if I have any to give?" I was uncomfortable revealing any weaknesses.

"No problem." she said.

It only took a few minutes for her to get the proper authorization from my doctor. I sat in the chair as she drew the required blood from my arm. Feeling relieved that I was being responsible. I thanked her and continued on with my work day.

It was early afternoon when I heard a knock on my door. This was odd. I was not to be bothered when I was with a client. I apologized to my client and stepped outside my room where Dr. Munsamy stood waiting. He looked at me confused and asked, "How are you doing it?"

Bewildered I asked, "What?"

He continued by telling me that my blood work was not good. He informed me that I shouldn't even have enough energy to walk, let alone be able to work.

"Oh," I said laughingly, "Coffee; that's the magic prescription. I drink a whole lot of coffee, it's all good." attempting to reassure him I was fine.

Not even humouring me with a smile, he asked, "What's wrong?"

I quieted my voice and told him I needed to finish with my client and then I would come talk to him. He would not hear of it. This made things difficult, we were friends first, then doctor patient, so I softly whispered "I think I need to see someone else for a bleeding problem".

He proposed I see a specialist immediately and asked if I needed an ambulance.

I laughed in amusement "I'm fine, I'll finish up my day with my clients that are booked, then we'll worry about this," reassuring him that all was well.

"That's not an option!" he insisted, adding, "You need to leave at once". With his adamant behaviour, it appeared that I had no choice.

I talked him into letting me finish the appointment that I was in the middle of. I also requested time to phone my clients to cancel the remainder of my day. Dr. Munsamy was not happy with me waiting an extra moment, but agreed reluctantly, as long as I saw the specialist right after. I nodded in agreement and did as I had promised.

Luckily I didn't have to worry about getting back in time for the bus. Amber and Michael spent Tuesday nights with their Dad. I was grateful not to have to worry about rearranging my childcare; one less issue to worry about.

The specialist I was to see was located in Carmen, a different rural hospital, an hour and fifteen minutes North West of Emerson. When I arrived for my appointment, I was thankful; I was going to get the quick fix needed to take care of this inconvenience.

Meeting with the surgeon was very matter-of-fact and not as uncomfortable as I had envisioned. Without buffering the results he said "You need surgery now."

Assuming that an oversight was made I calmly

responded, "That's not an option for me. I haven't the time for surgery. What are my alternatives?"

"None", he replied sombrely.

"Well, maybe I could make time in a few weeks," I said, trying to come up with a more workable plan.

The surgeon looked at me as if I was some brainless alien and stated seriously, "If you don't fix this right now, you won't be here in a few days. This is an emergency surgery, not an elective!"

Not fully realizing the severity of my situation, but sensing I again wasn't being given an option, I nervously responded in a light-hearted manner, "Well then, book me a pool side room."

The plans were in motion, the surgery was scheduled. My lack of blood made it mandatory that extra blood be readily available in case a transfusion would be required. This rural hospital did not have my type of blood on hand so the procedure was delayed until the following day. I asked if I could go home and wrap up a few things with work and the kids, and get some of my stuff. The surgeon reluctantly agreed, sternly telling me to arrive back early the following morning.

I did what I promised and arrived as requested the following day. As I waited impatiently for the surgery, they informed me that the extra blood had not arrived and the surgery would need to be rescheduled for the next morning. As I sat alone in the hospital that evening, the reality of what was happening began to take hold.

How could I have been so caught up in my day-to-day activities that I had neglected my health so severely? How could I have been in such denial? What had I been thinking? I had inadvertently taken a stressful situation and made it worse. This wasn't fair to the people in my life, especially my innocent children. The worst was the guilt. My need for denial put my children at risk of losing their mother.

I sat up in my bed compelled by an over-powering urge to write my children a note in case the unthinkable happened and I did not survive the surgery. I had some napkins left over from supper which I used to write messages to my children. I began the first letter to my daughter, Amber.

Through tears of regret I wrote, *Amber, if you are reading this, I did not do this to you on purpose. I would not have chosen to leave you without a mother.* I tried to explain how my intentions had been to be a good example of a woman and a mother. I finished the note with a heavy heart *I'm so very sorry I can't be here with you as you grow into the beautiful woman I know you will become. Love forever, Momma.*

On a separate napkin I wrote another heartfelt apology, this time to my son, Michael. I began the note, *Michael, I wanted to protect you from the world and be your most enthusiastic cheerleader. If you are reading this I made a very bad decision and I am so very, very sorry. I believe in you! Love Mom.* As I wrote to my children, tears ran down my cheeks, my remorse was overwhelming.

Slowly and tenderly I folded the napkins as I prayed the messages would not have to be read. I gently kissed each napkin separately before I stashed them away.

In the darkness of the room that night, I silently vowed if I made it through this surgery, things would change.

My failure was obvious; I had not factored myself into my

own equation and in so doing, the biggest obstacle in my life turned out to be me. Wanting to create some degree of normalcy for my children through the tough family transition, I had compromised my very survival by ignoring myself.

When we become fixated on the small details, not keeping the big picture in perspective, we live only a partial existence. In order to gain the fullness of life we need to live consciously. That means, taking a good look at what we are running from. This is mandatory if we are ever going to rise above our failures and grow to a stronger healthier self.

My need to believe failure was not an option had blinded me. I was in complete denial about the possibility of failure. I only permitted myself to see what I considered essential. I refused to acknowledge anything else because it didn't fit into the picture that I had created. I did not want to acknowledge the signs of failure nor was I fully aware of the possibly deadly ramifications of denial.

"It is we who have put our hands before our eyes and cry that it is dark."

~ Swami Vivekananda

Growth through Failure

Often our first response to failure is avoidance. Time and time again, through closer observation, we realize the valuable insights and wisdom attained through our past experiences with failure. With that said, rather than wait for the reflection of the experience in order to see the value in a failure, shouldn't we be looking for insight immediately?

Hidden silently within our failures are opportunities for acceptance and immediate enlightenment. Even when failure creates difficulties and setbacks, we should remind ourselves that we need these experiences for developing our strength, endurance, character etc...

Failure provides you with the opportunity to review aspects of yourself that you might have neglected. You will become stronger and wiser if you are willing to ask yourself questions like: Why? Why did I do this? What can I change? How can I learn...?

You will increase the speed of your development with awareness, acceptance, and the willingness to change what is not working for you. So let's get on this... the sooner the better!

"Be not ashamed of mistakes and thus make them crimes."

~ Confucius

Learning Process

Resisting the learning process is as futile as fighting the law of gravity. If we were to step out of a window, we would fall because the pull of gravity is inevitable. We recognize that we cannot fight the law of gravity; we accept it as part of life. We need to view failure in this same manner.

We use gravity to our benefit, why can't we view failure in that same fashion? I don't know anyone who likes to fail, but it's part of learning. I don't know anyone who likes to fall, but it's part of gravity. Our energy would be better utilized identifying what we stand to gain.

By accepting failure objectively, we gain access to a surplus of options. By doing this, we are able to take the constructive actions necessary for success. Let's continue learning, growing, understanding, experiencing, and living through failure, not seeking the absence of it.

"Failure is only the opportunity to begin again, only this time more wisely."

~ Henry Ford

Recognizing Abilities

Unfortunately, while trying to blend into our environment, we often ignore our natural guidance system. A lot of our gifts and talents go undiscovered and therefore underdeveloped because we are unaware of them.

Our natural aptitudes reveal themselves through our distinctive qualities; the free flowing talents we make appear effortless. They are as natural as our laughter and come as easily as breathing (for those of you who find breathing easy).

In order to fully blossom, we need to take advantage of the resources within us. Everyone is born with unique natural abilities. Discovering them will help guide you toward your passion and purpose.

Also, through reflection, you can understand why things in the past may not have worked. Knowing your gifts and abilities is only the beginning. When you accept your unique qualities you move into the path that is best suited to you.

Take the time to recognize and acknowledge what your particular talents are. Determine your specific talents so you can recognize them. And then build on them; use them to your greatest advantage.

When people say, you are not living up to your full potential, they are seeing things in you that you don't see; talents you may not be aware of and may not be utilizing.

Identifying your own abilities and special gifts is sometimes difficult. Once you recognize them, you can use them, making your life easier. Years ago, I purchased a used sewing machine at a garage sale; the problem with this machine was that it only sewed in reverse. Seeing the price was right and I was up for the challenge of sewing everything backwards, I bought it.

Manoeuvring my material unnaturally in reverse was more tedious, and a great deal more complicated than the natural forward direction in which it had been originally designed to function. Nearing the completion of my project, I accidently bumped a knob, previously broken on the front of the machine. To my delight, the machine started sewing forward with literally only the last few stitches needed to be completed on my project.

Needless to say, the last bit of stitching was surprisingly easier.

Yes, in hindsight, it would have made things easier if I'd stumbled upon this simple solution sooner, having the benefits of a normal sewing experience. Yes, it was a bit embarrassing to realize that I failed to recognize something so simple...but I didn't know.

What if you are stuck in reverse and all you need to do is simply push a button to make your life easier? If this is the case, how do you get unstuck? To start with, what abilities do you have that you may not be using? What talents do you have, or did you have that, for whatever reason, you stopped using?

Maybe you need to question whether those abilities are

salvageable. Maybe all you need to do is critique them just a little? Some of those abilities you have labelled as inabilities might only need a few minor adjustments to make them work for you. Looking inward at what you have to bring to the table is very important. We often do not realize what strengths we possess.

Talents are like muscles that need be developed through training and practice to help them grow. As you encourage your natural talents they will become more polished. This will help expand your opportunities for using the gifts that you were ultimately born to use.

A carpenter will often say he is only as good as his tools; however, this statement is not fully accurate. It does make it easier when we use the properly designed equipment, but the carpenter's understanding of his previous projects has developed skills within him that could never be extracted from just the tools themselves.

In this analogy, the tools the carpenter is using are the natural gifts we are given. The skills that he has developed through working are due to the knowledge he has obtained.

"Knowing others is wisdom, knowing yourself is enlightenment."

~ Tao Tzu

Failing to use Intuition

Within the many gifts we are born with are our instincts. Why would we have instincts if we were meant to disregard them?

We might not be aware that our instincts are one of the resources we possess within us. Or we might not recognize the importance of these distinctive gifts.

Without exception, we have all done things that we instinctively knew that we shouldn't do, but proceeded with anyway, against our better judgment.

This next story is one of my teenage lessons…

Against all Instincts

He frequented the restaurant where I worked. He came in like clockwork; one meal a day, every day. He had not missed a day in the three months I had been waitressing. His voice was muffled and uncertain when he spoke. He always ordered the same meal, day in and day out.

He always came in after the lunch crowd, but before the supper rush. His nervous responses made serving him awkward. He rarely made eye contact. As time went by I became accustomed to his nervousness.

Despite our limited communication I learned a number of facts about him: He lived alone. He flew a plane. He worked at the local Manitoba Hydro company.

The owner of the restaurant was a natural people

person. She knew how to make everyone feel welcome. Because he was such a regular, she insisted that he sit at the staff table, closest to the kitchen in order to get the quickest and best service. He always came in to the restaurant alone. He appeared to have no friends or family. I couldn't put my finger on it, but I had a sense of unease when I served him.

After months of serving this solitary middle aged man, he offered to take me for a flight in his plane. He knew, through one of our brief conversations, that I'd never flown in a plane before. Even though his offer was a generous one, I declined.

Later that shift, I mentioned the conversation to my boss who promptly responded, "Connie! You would be an idiot not to take advantage of this incredible opportunity." I was sorry that I had told her and didn't say anymore. The thought of being alone with this guy made me very uncomfortable.

The following day, he came in as usual. My boss, who meant well, decided to take matters into her own hands, against my wishes, and negotiated the details of the plane ride. It was settled! In two days, the following Sunday, I would experience the exhilaration of flight.

One of my co-workers, an older waitress, who seemed to share my discomfort with this arrangement, suggested we meet up with her family at their cabin at Rock Lake, for a picnic. Rock Lake was about a two hour drive away, a twenty five minute flight.

I could feel my heart pounding as we walked around the tiny two-seater Cessna airplane, doing the preliminaries together. To make matters worse, I couldn't see much of anything. Weeks earlier, at a healing service at our church, I had been told that, if I didn't want to wear glasses anymore, all I would need to do was remove them and my eyes would be healed. Well... this wasn't working for me. Weeks had passed and I was still as *blind as a bat*. Because I didn't want people in the church to think I didn't have faith, I was blindly walking around without my glasses.

After brief preliminaries and against my better judgment, it was time to climb into the plane with this guy.

The conversation was clumsy. I was sixteen, he was in his forties. There I sat, shoulder to shoulder with a fellow who wasn't even comfortable with himself. It was like pulling teeth to talk to this guy with other people around, and now I had been thrust into spending some one-on-one time with him in the air. *What was I thinking?*

The plane rolled into position. The nose pointed down the runway. We started moving forward, rapidly picking up speed, moving faster toward the end of the airstrip and then we lifted off the ground.

Soon after reaching the desired altitude, the plane settled. I breathed a sigh of relief while my body remained tense. I tried to relax. I needed to make the best of this uncomfortable situation. I stared out the window. The bird's eye view was wasted on me since I was not wearing my glasses. Everything below was blurred; patches of color blending together. Yes, I thought to myself this was an experience, *can we go home now?*

The plane seemed suspended motionless in the sky, as if the ground below was moving and not us. Shoulder to shoulder, neither of us spoke. I looked out my window into nothingness.

After about ten minutes into our flight I felt a hand on my knee. A sense of anxiety flooded my body. I could not help but acknowledge him. I turned to look at him. He was grinning from ear to ear. This was extremely unnerving as I had never seen this man smile before.

His eyes darted back and forth along the dashboard. He moved his hand slowly from my knee and placed it back on the steering column. He looked at me to see if I was watching him.

He giggled at my discomfort as he moved his hands into the air. My eyes became fixated on the steering mechanism. The steering mechanism was without human direction. *I didn't know a person could fly a plane hands free.* I nervously responded to his disturbing actions with a nod. I turned to stare back out my window in hope that I could make the moment go away.

I concentrated on the clouds through the glass in the door. *Please let this be a nightmare.* Moments passed. I was glad that was out of his system.

A tug on my seat belt pulled me from my inner monologue back into reality. I turned to see what he was doing. He was bent sideways toward me, his eyes locked on mine, his hand resting on my hip as he pulled on my seat belt.

"Do you know what kind of control I have?" he asked.

My mind searched for something to say as he repeated his statement. "I don't need my hands to fly this plane."

My heart sank. Uncomfortable thoughts raced through my mind as helplessness enveloped me. I remained silent, my eyes pleaded, *Please don't hurt me.* He stared forward as his hand slid along the edge of my seat belt, which lay across my chest.

"Just want to make sure you are wearing your seat

belt. Who knows? Maybe your door might open accidentally," He said with an awkward snicker. He slowly reached his hand past me, brushing his arm against my body. And then, he opened my door.

Shock flooded through me. My thoughts disappeared with the wind and the noise and visions of horrific possibilities. I sat frozen, waiting to see what he would do next. I stared forward. I didn't know what to do. I didn't know how to respond to his actions... so I didn't. After what seemed to be forever, he reached back over me and closed my door. He laughed nervously. Silently, we continued the flight.

My uneasy response, my pleading silent prayers, my unseen angel must have saved me from the possibilities. Thankfully, I had been fortunate... this time.

Looking at the basics of this situation, I had ignored my primary instincts. Adding to this failure, even with my instincts ringing loud enough for the neighbourhood to hear, I didn't have the self-confidence to trust my intuition... Double whammy!!

Ever since that experience I have worn my indispensable glasses.

"Success is going from failure to failure without losing your enthusiasm."

~ Abraham Lincoln

Self Confidence

All of us came into this world with self-confidence. Through the process of growing up, we have allowed others to take some of our confidence away. As others reveal their warped reflections of our less than perfect selves, we tend to lose more confidence. Being introduced to failure at an early age quickly teaches us to feel inferior and inadequate before our inborn confidence has an opportunity to become stronger. Whether we acknowledge it or not, we are influenced by what other people think or say about us; some people more than others.

When we are young, our parents are the strongest influences in our lives. If a parent says we are no good we don't hear those words as just attitude, we take ownership of them. It's quite possible that our personalities were shaped out of fear, fear of not fitting in, fear of failure, fear of being rejected.

As we grow up, we are introduced to an assortment of opinions. We are rarely conscious of the choice we have to either receive or reject the opinions of others before adopting them as our own. When we take what someone thinks or says about us and value it more than our own awareness of Truth, we undermine our base confidence.

Self-confidence is based on knowledge of our Truth. Our judgments are built on concepts that we have created through objective feedback. Our worth and value are gathered from the tiny fragments of information that we have obtained from various people and circumstances.

If we bear in mind that our perceptions could be inaccurate, we open up more possibilities. By understanding that how we view ourselves is a matter of perception, we gain the ability to alter that belief. We become free to change with the realization that we are the ones who created this idea in the first place.

Consequently, when you change your character-limiting beliefs, recognizing your worth, you allow yourself the freedom to step outside the views you previously held about yourself.

Self-confidence is based on how we view ourselves. If we're going to overcome insecurities and succeed at being authentic, we can't continue to be afraid of what everybody else may think. We shouldn't allow others to fit us into their moulds. With the assistance of strong self-confidence, we can, and should embrace our differences. We are all unique!

"Every adversity, every failure, every heartache carries with it the seed of an equal or greater benefit."

~ Napoleon Hill

Reprogramming

Positive sustainable change can only take place when you seek out Truth, having the willingness and the courage to take that hard honest look at yourself. Seek out Truth, not your perceived reality, not others' reality, but true unadulterated reality. Look into yourself; shine the light of Truth upon your idealized illusions. Accept your inadequacies. You have the power to fix them.

Around the age of eight, I learned the proper pronunciation of the letter "R" by just this method. I had come home from a mentally exhausting day in grade two and was tearfully explaining to my mother the hopelessness of my situation.
She calmly asked me if I really wanted to learn.
I started crying and said, "Not if it's going to hurt."
My mom pulled out a hand mirror and asked me to repeat after her the sound, "Rrrrr". As I did this, she pointed out that I was not rolling my tongue as she was in order to get the sound I was seeking. I looked back in the mirror and saw something I had not seen before: My incorrect positioning of my tongue. With this new found insight, within a very short time I was repeating the sound properly.

The mirror of Truth does not lie. With this Truth, comes freedom for change. We can easily develop new habits if we become aware of the bad habits that need altering. If we are willing to take the tough step of looking at our true reflection, we can alter our life in a phenomenally, almost inconceivable manner.

What is it about failure that scares us? Failure is unavoidable. This very thing we fear is the gold that paves the way towards our success. Have you ever heard of someone who achieves success without having made any prior mistakes? The natural progression to reach your dreams is failing through the process. Value this natural law. Embrace it as part of your journey.

"The world we see that seems so insane is the result of a belief system that is not working. To perceive the world differently, we must be willing to change our belief system, let the past slip away, expand our sense of now, and dissolve the fear in our minds."

~ William James

Mistaken Identity

People who are successful at working through failure don't blame themselves or others when they fail. They take responsibility for each setback. And... they do not take failure personally. Failure is temporary and needs to be worked through just as any good learning process.

Speaking of people...

Hidden amongst the rubble of our minds are collections of facts and data about other people and their apparent identities. Through our evaluation process, we inevitably miss some essential facts about people while developing our own opinions. Occasionally, after analyzing things in a more subjective way, we can see that our thoughts about someone or something were not accurate.

This next failure in my life had to do with me needing to believe things about people; the good of mankind, idealistically seeing only what I wanted to see,

It was the end of October, 1989. My husband, Jeff, and I were frantically getting everything ready for the Grand Opening of our first retail store. The smell of fresh paint permeating the room reassured us of all the work that had already been done. The over-flowing boxes that dominated the floor reminded us of all the work that still remained.
The soon to open 'Music Shoppe' had the young people in Altona buzzing with anticipation. We had covered the display windows, and the sliding glass doors that faced

the inside of the mall with thick brown paper to add to the intrigue and excitement.

During the course of the past month, we had met many of the youth who curiously poked their heads into the store to introduce themselves, hoping to get an inside scoop of the renovation.

This particular evening my husband was worn out and had called it a day. I, on the other hand was determined to get more accomplished before allowing exhaustion to overtake me. It was almost 9:00 p.m. and the shopping centre was preparing to close. As usual, I could hear through the glass door, some of the teens talking and laughing in the mall. After overhearing their enthusiastic energy, I had a brilliant idea.

I opened the heavy covered glass door, just enough to poke my head into the hallway. I waved to the group of teenagers to come closer. Animatedly, I asked them if any of them wanted to trade their time for music. All four boys eagerly agreed.

From the corner of my eye, I noticed a well-dressed young man leaning against the far wall. His arms crossed. He appeared to be studying the movements of his surroundings. I motioned for him to also join us. The group of teenagers immediately tried to discourage me with their obvious stares of disapproval, trying to convey the message that this was not a good idea. I ignored their adverse reactions thinking it was just a *clique* thing.

I energetically introduced myself and asked the teenagers their names. The guys all reciprocated except the loner. He seemed hesitant in giving me any information about himself, including his name. He paused and then self-confidently introduced himself as Earl.

Because it was a school night we all agreed that the evening would not be a long one. The teenagers rummaged through the discount bins and took the recorded cassette they wanted in return for their efforts. They eagerly began their assigned tasks.

Less than a half-hour into the arranging of the cassettes and cd's, I excused myself to use the washroom that was located in the middle of the mall. When I returned, just a few moments later, only Earl, the young man who had been in the shadows, the loner in the hall, remained.

"Where did everyone go?" I asked.

The young man replied in a matter of fact tone, "It was late, the boys needed to go home." Perplexed by their sudden urgency to leave I looked down at my watch. We still had almost an hour before the 10:30 curfew. Sensing my bewilderment he reassured me, "Don't worry, I locked the mall door behind them."

Dead silence filled the room. What just happened was unsettling.

I was confused. Nevertheless, I decided to set my feelings aside and focus on the work that needed doing. I broke the silence by saying, "Thank you, I'm glad you thought of that."

We went back to the spots we had been prior to my bathroom break. We continued the tedious job the group had started of transferring the recorded music into the plastic sleeves designed for theft prevention.

As we sat on the floor on opposite corners of the display rack, we began to talk.

The conversation took the tone of question and answer: I asked, he answered. All his answers seemed deliberate and calculated. I could tell that this young 16 year old was extremely bright, very articulate, unlike most his age. He had a very confident, almost arrogant demeanour.

After working for about 10 minutes, I realized he was still wearing his heavy outdoor jacket. I casually said, "It's pretty warm in here, why don't you take your jacket off?" He ignored me as if I hadn't spoken. In the awkward silence, we continued working.

I allowed a few moments to pass before I decided to repeat myself, thinking maybe he hadn't heard me. He appeared annoyed. Again, he refused to acknowledge that I had said anything. I didn't understand his obvious frustration with my suggestion. Concerned about his comfort, I questioned him once again, "Aren't you too hot in your jacket?" He stood to his feet and left the store without a word.

I was shocked and confused at his response, however, my need to remain focused on my project took over my attention as I continued with what needed doing.

* * * *

The *Music Shoppe* opened as planned on November 1st. During this time, and not exactly as planned, after six years of marriage, I became pregnant. Not yet aware of this, we continued to operate the store. We were the staff.

Because I was always at the store, I became friends with the teens who floated in and out, including the eccentric young loner, Earl, who was now seventeen. He would come by and visit with me almost every day.

One thing I noticed about Earl was that he didn't appear to have any friends. I couldn't understand why. I saw so much potential in him. Nevertheless, the aversion between him and the outside world was obvious, especially when he entered the store. Everyone, including the adults would physically separate themselves from him, like oil and water.

Over time, I become more aware of Earl's strange mannerisms. I reasoned that his abnormal behaviour was normal...for him. Some days, he would purposely come into the store to see if he could un-nerve me. He would hint that I should not leave my car door unlocked. He would also remind me that people should lock their doors to their houses too, insinuating that he had been inside my home.

I had no reaction to his need to try to control with fear and intimidation. *The games of a teenage boy,* I rationalized.

I felt close to him like an older sister would. When he came into the store I found myself enjoying his company. He was close to my younger brother Robert's age and because of this, I asked him to watch out for Robert in the high school and not be one of his problems as I heard he had a tendency to be.

Months passed. When Earl found out that I was pregnant he was not happy and did not try to hide his disapproval. His reaction puzzled me. I assured him that I would continue working in the store for at least five more months and that we could still visit with each other. I gave no thought to him as anything more than a young friend. I was married, very religious, twenty four, and pregnant.

During this time, my husband became more and more irritated with Earl's attitude. He was annoyed by a combination of things concerning Earl. He did not appreciate the disruption Earl created within our store.

I understood from the perspective of shop owner that we needed to handle the situation, as it was starting to affect our business. Jeff also did not like the vibe he felt from Earl.

One day, my husband walked through the store while Earl and I were casually talking. Jeff expressed his disapproval of Earl wasting my time. Earl casually looked over at Jeff and hinted about the tires on our car going flat. That was it, Jeff had enough of the young man's attitude and in an angry outburst, banned Earl from ever entering the *Music Shoppe*.

* * * *

As time went by, Earl coincidently bumped into me more and more in the mall. When this happened, he would walk with me as I did my shopping. He often joined me for my coffee breaks. We talked about life, goals and aspirations. Because of my thinking like the older sister, I tried to encourage him in the right direction.

What I found strange was his continued questioning of why I was not scared of him, since he felt that power over everyone else. I would reiterate my response in similar way, "You don't scare me and you might as well stop trying to manipulate me with fear, I'm not afraid of you." However, in reality, I was a little uncomfortable about what others were saying about him.

One of the more disturbing rumours involving Earl was a specific local break-and-enter. Rumour was that Earl had snuck into a prominent businessman's home and had taken two pictures from the family's photo album: A picture of their daughter and a picture of their son. In the spot where one picture had been, an unsettling note was left in its place. The note described what might happen to the children if the family contacted the police. The photo albums had been tucked away in their living room, in the privacy of their home.

Altona was a small Mennonite community. We didn't feel the need to lock our doors...sadly that changed soon after.

During one of our many conversations, I asked Earl, "What do you want to be when you grow up?"

He revealed that he wanted to either become a lawyer or a contract killer. I laughed and strongly recommended him choosing the lawyer-route, as the other option shouldn't be a consideration. He would try to describe in detail how it would feel to kill someone. Whenever he starting talking like that, I would stop his words in disgust, reprimanding him, "Don't say that!"

I believed, at the time that he was merely seeking another way to get attention. Yes, I had heard about his break-and-enters, some of his threats to people in our community, his apparent addiction to creating fear within others, but I knew a different boy, a boy who just wanted to be noticed. I did not believe I was being blind to what I heard or saw. I thought, somehow, that I could be the facilitator to change his perception, to make him realize that he didn't need to do those things to be accepted...but this was not meant to be.

This story does not end well. The young man is serving a life sentence for the horrific crimes he subsequently committed. He was convicted of murder of a young man and attempted murder of another.

Our lives continued to overlap during the court hearings and the trial. Within this life lesson is much sadness and pain that I will not go into at this time. I was not a target of what transpired, but I was painfully affected by my inability to alter that future… that has now become the past.

"No amount of guilt can change the past and no amount of worrying change the future."

~ Umar Ibn al-Khattab

Not Guilty

Many people's lives were changed because of one man's actions. The sad reflection from those days contributes to the all-consuming guilt that many carry due to what this young man did. So many innocent people were affected, taking on their own private guilt for something they could not control; guilt they should not own. Because of what happened that tragic day, many lives were changed forever.

Personally, this has been one of my hardest battles of *what if? What if I would have...? I should have...?* Shame for not knowing, replaying in my mind what should have been done. *What if?* How we view our part in any tragedy can create unbearable guilt regardless of whether it is, justifiable or not.

Shame makes us internalize, convincing ourselves that we are bad, or that we are incapable of doing anything right as we continue to punish ourselves for past failures. This kind of guilt is never-ending as we silently blame ourselves for crimes we did or did not commit. We subconsciously punish ourselves for our past involvement of a tragedy; guilty or not.

We can feel guilty about virtually anything. This emotion knows no time limit. We can feel guilt over something which happened twenty five years ago, as is the case with Earl, the convicted murderer, or we can allow ourselves to feel this way about something that hasn't even happened yet. This is unhealthy. We all currently suffer or have suffered from this type of emotional pain.

Some believe that by continuing to feel guilty that they are doing something to rectify a situation. These people believe feeling this emotion makes them good people. They believe, with some faint, faulty, familiar memory, there's something good about feeling bad, even though they may no longer remember why… How sad is that?

Take responsibility and then… let go of the guilt

The way to stop the cycle of guilt involves re-training ourselves to replace our feeling with knowledge of responsibility. The first step is to become aware of exactly what we are feeling guilty about. When we are feeling badly about something, we need to ask ourselves if we are indeed guilty of something. Is there something we should feel guilty about? What is triggering this feeling? This reaction might only be based in habit, not reality.

The second step is to realize that we have a choice on how to respond. We don't have to feel guilty. If we make a mistake at work, for instance, instead of feeling guilty we can fix the problem, and then figure out a way to prevent that mistake, or a similar one, from happening again.

When you feel guilt, say sorry for what you did because you are sorry…and then let go of the guilt. When you feel guilty about something where you need to apologize and make amends, do that! The other person will feel better and so will you. If you feel guilty about something that happened a long time ago and it doesn't appear amends can be made, it may help to alleviate some of your guilt to accept that you genuinely feel apologetic and have learned through the experience. This will help your negative feelings diminish and disappear.

Writing a letter, indicating what you are sorry for and promising never to do it again, is a good way to let go of guilt. You can then burn the letter or create a personal ceremony of your intentions. Let go of what you no longer have control over.

This kind of action can be a powerful way of releasing the bonds of guilt. Maybe it's time to write a forgiving letter. Maybe that letter needs to be written to you? When you write such a letter, you need to be sensitive and write it with much love, warmth and appreciation for yourself. Write to someone who is a good, kind and worthy person, who is not perfect but accepted none-the-less.

We are all imperfect! Every one of us! The sooner you embrace yourself as being fallible, the easier it will be to fully love and accept yourself. This releases your need for perfection and will teach you compassion for yourself and for others. The more you can appreciate how wonderful you are, the more difficult it will be to beat yourself up for past failures. Once you have dealt with the past, you can free yourself from the guilt and move forward.

"One of the hardest lessons in life is letting go. Whether it's guilt, anger, love, loss or betrayal. Change is never easy. We fight to hold on and we fight to let go."

~ *Unknown*

Through The Process

Growing through the process of life can be challenging. Remaining focused on the core of who you are is mandatory. It is important to remember to take the lessons from any particular challenge and move on; changing directions if necessary. Take the priceless lessons from life, the good, the bad and the ugly. Learn from them... and move on.

Continue to pursue your goals. A change of mindset regarding mistakes, mishaps and misfortunes is compulsory in order to grow upward and onward. Reject rejection!

Courage and effort is what life's challenges demand. With your strong attributes in place, you can reclaim the exceptional individual who is hiding scared within you. As long as you believe in a possibility, the possibility exists! If you allow yourself to grow wiser and stronger from setbacks, you will become more confident and secure in your ability to not just survive, but thrive!

You will never truly know yourself until you have been tested by adversity, so move forward toward the challenges. Accept the hardships and failures that await you.

Our process

Have an experience
Think about the experience
Learn from the experience
Apply the knowledge

Love Forever

The aroma of fresh baking filled the air. I smiled as I ran around the apartment thinking to myself, I'm so lucky; I didn't expect to see her until Christmas!

My daughter, Amber was settling into her second year of university in Saskatoon, 780 kilometres west of her Winnipeg home, across the wide, flat Canadian prairies. The fall semester was the fourth time she had been away since she came into the world twenty-one years ago. I never worried that her travels would create a distance between us; our bond was unbreakable. The thought of seeing her again made my heart sing. Even though I had seen her less than two weeks earlier, I missed her.

Amber had phoned me a few days earlier to let me know of her possible plans. She laughed nervously as she shared her thoughts about, maybe, coming home for the weekend. I grinned broadly as I recognized that she was seeking my approval in her decision. She began by saying, "I can't miss Grandpa's 70th birthday celebration!" And then, with hardly a breath or pause she went into detail about how she needed to catch up with Grandma and snuggle with Chloe, their most recent puppy addition. She went on and on about how important family was to her and how much she missed everyone. She quickly added, "Even auntie Shannon, from Toronto is going to be there." Amber giggled as she talked about holding her baby nephew, Oliver, in her arms. "How can I not come home?" she excitedly declared, as she chuckled with delight. Her mind was made up. I laughed; I knew I couldn't talk her out of it, nor did I want to. I had been spoiled during the last summer break by having her around more than usual. I missed her.

Our Thanksgiving weekend was going to be extra special. It was Friday and my Amber was on her way home! Looking around my apartment, I was pleased. Everything was ready! I had recently moved into a beautiful 17th floor apartment with a spectacular view of the city skyline and the wide prairies beyond. It was a west-facing view allowing me to take in the gorgeous long sunsets. It also faced the direction from which Amber would be driving home. That gave me comfort, as if I could somehow watch over her just a bit sooner than her arrival.

Expecting her to be tired after her long drive, I prepared a comfortable bed for her on the couch. When I was finished, I plopped myself down beside the blankets. What a wonderful weekend it will be! My mind wandered to where she might be on her journey home. I could hardly wait to hold her in my arms!

She had texted me in the late afternoon to say that her departure had been delayed. She would be arriving home around midnight. I texted back, *No worries...drive safely.* The afternoon turned to evening and soon it was midnight. I wasn't worried. She had texted me at 8:20 in the evening loling. She had forgotten about the time change and would be an hour later than planned. I texted her back: *Keep driving safe...no rush.*

I lay on the couch as the time ticked by. My thoughts turned to Amber and how fortunate I was to have such an unusually close relationship with her. I thought about how we had worked through the classic mother/daughter conflicts that typify the teenage years. I marvelled at how we were always able to talk heart-to-heart. I knew that this next year would be even more transformative as my Amber was indeed a beautiful young woman. I took a deep breath in as I recognized that my baby girl would never return the same innocent child who wandered through the meadows on Grandma and Grandpa's farm catching butterflies, but a grown woman who will undoubtedly be metamorphosed by her continued experiences.

My thoughts drifted to our most recent trip together, less than two weeks earlier; what an enjoyable getaway it had been. A last minute surprise for Amber, I had arranged her flight from Saskatoon to meet me in Las Vegas to celebrate her 21st birthday. We spent four of the most wondrous days and nights together, being mother and daughter... and best of friends.

The minutes ticked by without any further word from Amber. I was getting anxious but I calmed myself as I was just being my motherly self; there was nothing to fear. I decided to text her around 1 a.m. *Hey baby girl, have you arrived in Winnipeg?* I thought about these words carefully before I pressed send. I didn't want her to think I was either annoyed or distressed. She didn't text me back. That wasn't like her. I hated to admit it, but I was worried. Just after 3 a.m., I texted her again in a more desperate tone, *Hey Amber...Is everything ok?*

As I lay on the couch, wrapped up in the blankets I'd prepared for her arrival, my mind wandered to the unthinkable. Needing reassurance, I reluctantly phoned a friend, an RCMP officer who happened to be the head of the local highway patrol. There was no answer. I didn't leave a message as I felt foolish to be bothering him. I assured myself that if something had happened, someone would have contacted me. I decided that she must have gotten a bit tired and did the right thing by pulling over to take a nap.

Waiting in the darkness, my thoughts became more occupied on all the negative possibilities. I didn't know what to do. Apprehensively, I again phoned my friend. After a few rings, he answered. I apologized for calling so late and then quickly told him that Amber had not arrived as planned. As calmly as I could, I slowly asked, "Has anyone reported a car accident?" I told him which highway she had intended to take. He said he would check and call me back. He called back just minutes later saying no accident had been reported. I was relieved, but still worried. I felt helpless. I really couldn't do anything until the morning if she didn't arrive. The sense of each moment was heightened by the situation and every little thing, every heartbeat, every thought became significant. I wanted so much for that sound in the hallway to be Amber.

The night did not want to end. As I lay waiting, I thought about the last time I saw my Amber. We were in the Las Vegas airport. Amber was flying back to Saskatoon to school; I was flying back to Winnipeg. A friend of mine, who lives in Vegas, had picked us up from our hotel to drive us to the airport. On the way, he took us for one last photo op, as he laughingly called it, in front of the world-famous Welcome to Las Vegas sign before dropping us off at the airport.

At the airport we were both going through the normal motions of getting our bags checked in, tickets confirmed and passports in order. I was trying to be as focused as possible, as if it would, somehow, delay the inevitable moment at hand. I had turned to put the stickers onto her luggage when she ran up behind me and gave me one of her *famous-arms-wrapped-around-me-from-the-back-hugs*. Sadly it was time to say goodbye.

Amber looked directly at me and started to cry. "I don't think I can wait until Christmas to see you again".

I tried to be logical, strong and motherly as I wrapped my arms around her, pulling her in as I held her as close as possible. I softly whispered in her ear, "Time is only but a moment Amber, we'll soon be together once again." I gently guided her face toward mine. I looked deeply in her eyes as I wiped away her tears. "I love you so much Amber." Tears continued to stream down her cheeks as she said she couldn't imagine her life without me. She pulled me closer, even tighter, sobbing, "I love you So-Oo much." Caught up in the overwhelming emotion of love, now I was the one with tears streaming down my cheeks. Our eyes softly locked. In that moment, I caught the reflection of my own love shining back upon me.

Unwillingly, we finally let go of each other and said our last goodbye. I watched her slowly rise up the escalator as she smiled through her tears. She glanced down at her feet and then back to me as she waved goodbye. As she looked at me, I blew a kiss toward her. She wiped away her tears. She smiled and took her hand and blew a kiss back to me. I felt so much love, so much joy, and so much pride in that instant. And then she was gone. As I walked toward my departure gate I couldn't help reflect on how Amber's love and attention to me had been extra intense, as if she was saying it for the last time.

Overcome by my concern and worry, I picked up my cell phone. It was now half past 3 and no sign of Amber. I texted again: *I hate to admit it…But I am a little worried, is everything ok? When do you think you will be here?*

Time seemed to stand still. The darkness of the night was now yielding to the light of early morning. The stillness in my apartment echoed the feeling within me. I stared at my phone waiting… willing for a reply. An hour had passed since I last texted her. Instinctively, reluctantly, I couldn't hide my worry as I texted: *Amber, could you give me a sign that you're ok…Please…*

    I lay there for another hour or so, not moving, but not sleeping either, physically drained from my thoughts. It was full daylight now. I didn't bother to look at the clock. Trying to make sense of Amber's scheduled arrival with the numbers on the clock was just too much to think about. Everything was out of time.

    I began to fold the blankets that were supposed to be for Amber when the phone rang. I half expected what happened next. It was my friend, the RCMP officer wanting to know my daughter's license plate number. Distracted, apprehensive and trembling inside but not wanting to display my emotions, I told him, "I don't know, I just re-insured the car last week, I'll call you right back with that information." Minutes later I made the call with her plate number.

    "Thanks," he said and hung up.

    My RCMP friend took on the role of middle man when it came to relaying the news that followed. On the next call he said Amber's car was found in the ditch about two hours north west of Winnipeg. It appeared she had opened the door and was not in the vehicle. The call was brief. My fears were confirmed. Amber had been in an accident. However, it wasn't the worst news, Amber will be okay, I told myself…*she's a survivor.*

    Consumed by my responsibility to find my daughter, I starting calling all the hospitals in the area to see if anybody had been admitted that night; but none of them had my Amber. I felt so helpless. I could do nothing but wait. My fears were taking over.

Because the car was confirmed to be Amber's, I called her Dad. After updating Jeff, he insisted I tell our son what was happening. I heard Jeff bang on the bedroom door to wake up our 19 year old son who was temporarily staying with him. I didn't want to tell Michael like this, but was given no choice.

After he picked up the phone I apologized for waking him. I calmly told him what was happening; that nothing was confirmed and I would keep him updated. Shaken but hopeful, I hung up and moved on. I proceeded to call my mom to tell her the news. She said she would pray.

Moments after I hung up with my mom, the phone rang again. It was my RCMP friend to say he had been ill-informed. The car had actually flipped and was sitting upside down in a ditch filled with water. They were waiting for a tow truck to pull it out. I painstakingly asked the next question. "Could they see if she was in the car?" He said he couldn't say, as they would not know until they pulled the car out of the water.

It seemed like a lifetime between updates, but it was, in fact only about an hour later that all the information necessary to know was relayed between the highway patrol, my RCMP friend and me.

The phone rang a little before 10 a.m. on that Saturday morning. The news was not good. They found my daughter. She was still inside the car. She was dead. My knees instantly became weak as I slowly sat myself down of the edge of the bed. In shock, I calmly apologized to my friend for having put him in this very difficult position of telling me and I thanked him again. I proceeded to ask some questions about what happened. He told me it appeared as though she swerved to avoid a deer and hit the ditch. The car rolled and landed upside down, crushing and flattening the roof of the car. He said, "By all appearances, she did not suffer as her head injuries were severe."

    I thanked him again and hung up. For a drawn out minute there was silence in the room except for the clock that ticked off the seconds. For twenty-one years and fourteen days it had ticked the intervals from the day of Amber's birth until this very moment.

    My eyes became fixated on my phone as if it was still an open connection to my Amber. I felt an overwhelming need to finish my conversation with my daughter, as I had been texting her throughout the night. I took the phone and with shaking fingers I texted her for the last time: *I love you* followed by the symbols of a kiss goodbye, a heart, and a broken heart. As I pressed send, the fact that this was the last message I would ever send to her hit me hard.

    There would be no more waiting, no more imposing a sense of urgency or concern on Amber's late arrival. My most unsettling fears had turned from stunned disbelief to unimaginable sorrow. I could no longer contain my pent-up emotions as tears streamed down my cheeks. I broke down temporarily but I soon realized that I had to continue to be strong...for Amber.

    I contacted Amber's dad, my son and my family. I phoned my daughter's boyfriend, leaving a message saying that he should phone me as soon as he could. I did not want him to hear the devastating news through Facebook or anyone else. When he called back about an hour later, I told him about the accident. He began to cry as he told me he shouldn't have let her go by herself. I told him that this was no one's fault. He was obviously distraught and could not remain on the phone.

The rest of that day was a blur. I went for a walk to clear my head. I needed to get out of the apartment before its association to the moment became too great. There was nothing more I could do. Even though I was exhausted as I had not slept that night, I was afraid to close my eyes. I was afraid to be disconnected from my new reality, an unimaginable reality that at some point I would need to face.

"Crying doesn't indicate that you are weak. Ever since you were born it's a sign that you are alive."

~ Unknown

Beauty within Ashes

Throughout Saturday the authorities were directly in touch with me; they told me that they had taken Amber's body from the accident scene to the nearest hospital. The coroner would send her on to Winnipeg as soon as they could arrange transport.

My mind searched for meaning as I tried to comprehend my immense loss.

My memories began to unfold as I reflected on the many conversations my daughter and I had philosophised on, including the inevitability of death.

One memory had particular relevance at this time. A few years earlier my Amber had gone to Ecuador as a volunteer with Canada World Youth. Her placement had been in a rural mountainous area, in a home of a local family. During her stay, an unfortunate accident took place. The incident altered Amber's conception of life and death.

The group of volunteers worked with some of the children in the area. One of the local boys, who spent much of his time with them, decided to take an afternoon break on his own to relax in his backyard. He assured the group that he would join them after a bit. It was okay. The boy's mom was inside. Everything was as it should be. However, when the group came back from their days activities, to their horror they found the young boy entangled lifelessly in the hammock in the yard behind the house.

Amber couldn't grasp the magnitude of what happened. In a blink of an eye, a young vibrant spirit was no longer among them. Life, for her, and those around her, had changed forever.

When Amber came back from Ecuador, she was different. She had attained wisdom through an experience that most eighteen year olds do not possess. She described to me the misfortunate accident in detail. She shared how it had affected her. Strangely, what stood out the most for her was not the death, but the way the culture handled the tragedy. It appeared to be the opposite to how our society handles the death of a child.

She elaborated on how the people from far and wide all gathered to celebrate the life of the young boy. Everyone wore bright and vibrant colours to symbolize the gift of the young boy's life, rejoicing in the luminous spirit that had blessed them with his presence. They danced in joyful celebration. I had asked about the parents and the family and the grief they must have suffered. She said it was not easy for the family to adjust to the loss, but there was a strange peaceful acceptance that surrounded the suffering.

This experience moved her to such a degree that she changed one of her university courses. Among her minor courses, she enrolled in funeral studies to help people grieve the loss of their loved ones.

* * * *

On Sunday, as originally planned, I went out to the country for our Thanksgiving gathering and my Dad's birthday celebration. I needed to be with my parents, my brothers and sisters, and their families. Amber would have wanted us to celebrate. That was not possible, of course. The mood was sombre, more like a wake or pre-funeral gathering. There were many tears. I did not stay long as Amber's body was to arrive in Winnipeg that afternoon.

Amber's dad and I were asked if one or both of us

could identify her body, so they could move forward with the autopsy. I felt strongly that I needed to see her one last time. Her father felt the opposite. He could not bear to face that vision, an understandable and equally valid response to the death of a child. We each deal with grief in different ways.

Later that afternoon we stood waiting in the cold sterile hallway of the hospital. I had brought my boyfriend with me for support. My ex-husband, Jeff brought his wife and both of his sisters. The medical examiner entered from the inside door. Without emotion, she introduced herself as she must have done with hundreds, perhaps thousands before us. She had seen it all and for her it was just another day of work. For me, her detachment was obvious and my heart wanted her, the doctor, to be more under-standing; this wasn't just anyone, this was my Amber.

She asked us to follow her. We were led down the long corridor toward the room where my daughter's body was waiting. She explained very matter-of-factly that they could not clean up the body because that would be tampering with evidence prior to an autopsy. She explained that because the car had been immersed in water, our daughter may be muddy and physically distorted. She also made it clear Amber's head injuries were severe and that she would have blood on her.

Deep down I knew that this was all happening, but something in me was hoping that there had been a terrible mix-up. That it wasn't going to be Amber. With all my heart I didn't want this to be the last time I would see her. I didn't want to say goodbye.

As we approached the room my knees went weak. I was no longer sure of my need for closure in this way. Jeff and I had both brought supportive people with us. I was assured that they could identify her, if we could not. I took a deep breath. I knew I had to see her for myself.

I was scared that my legs would give way. I asked my boyfriend if he could come in with me. He reminded me that I did not have to do this. My mind was clearly focused; I knew I had to do this for me.

As we entered the room, I saw her, my beautiful daughter. Her body lay quiet and still on the cold metal table, a white sheet draped over her body. Her head wrapped in a white towel just as she would have done after a shower. Her arms were placed gently upon her chest, her body motionless. I couldn't get over her incredible beauty "Oh my", I softly sobbed, "She's so beautiful."

Her face, her form was, without a doubt, my Amber. I couldn't get over how incredibly peaceful she appeared. I gasped for air in an involuntary reaction as I cried out loud. I deeply missed her. I couldn't take my eyes off of my Amber, especially her face. Her eyelashes appeared extra-long due to the mud that oddly highlighted her loveliness. Even though her lifeless corpse was just that, a dead human body, I marvelled at her incredible beauty, even in death. I was relieved that what the coroner had prepared me for was not what I saw. She was so beautiful.

My heart was torn. Part of me wanted to touch her; I wanted to wipe away the smears of dried mud on her cheek. But I didn't want to be left with the coldness of her vacant body as my last memory of touching her. That had been just two weeks earlier as we hugged at the Las Vegas airport.

Amber's body lay lifeless before me, the shell of where her spirit had once been. In that moment of realization, I felt so thankful that she had shared her life with us. It had been an honour to have been the one person on earth who could proudly say, I was her mom.

Now, as if her spirit was waiting for me to say good bye, I could feel her join with me. She was not within this empty vessel in front of us any longer. The feeling of peace enveloped me as I gazed at her beauty.

During a brief reflective moment, my heart rose above the grief that the others were feeling as I remembered the promise of those last words that will echo in my heart forever, *Time is only but a moment and we'll soon be together once again.* And so we are.

* * * *

Amber's spirit would have danced at her memorial celebration. We asked those who attended to wear bright colours to mirror her vibrant spirit. Many of her friends wore purple, her favourite colour. I was at peace in my sadness.

"Life is a series of experiences, each one of which makes us bigger, even though sometimes it is hard to realize this. For the world was built to develop character, and we must learn that the setbacks and grieves which we endure help us in our marching onward."

~ Henry Ford

Facing Reality

I would love to conclude that *only* rainbows and butterflies followed me through my healing process, but that would be far from the truth. Coming to grips with the loss of a loved one is not as easy as accepting that we must fail in order to succeed. Dealing with grief is difficult.

We can try to make light of it or we can try to hide from it, but only until it hits us where it hurts.

Sooner or later, each of us will experience that dagger in the heart called grief. One thing true about life is that nobody gets out alive. Because of this, we all have or will have to deal with the trauma of losing someone we love; someone we thought we would or could never live without.

Everyone grieves in their own unique way. The question then becomes, *how?* How do you pick up the pieces left after a loss? How do you heal emotional wounds? How do you move on without feeling like you're betraying the memory of your loved one?

Working through grief is a challenge like no other. Dealing effectively with grief is crucial to the recovery process. It is essential to deal with the grief of any loss if we are to regain the ability to continue with and fulfill our life purpose.

You might think that because my life had been filled with so many unforeseen hardships and challenges that I would have been able to grow through this life experience at a remarkable speed. Or, because I believe all experiences have wisdom hidden within, that I would have been able to magically transcend the pain of my loss?

This was not the case, nor would it have been good for me. Like it or not, this was a part of my life story. When we face a personal loss, we find out a lot about ourselves. We find out if we have been just saying things, or if we really believe them.

Luckily for me, because I truly believe everything, somehow, someway works out, I didn't fight my pain. Through the toughest part of the transition, I had faith that I would emerge from the darkness that accompanied my grief, and I did. I'm not saying that I didn't question: *Why; Why me? Why her? Why now?* Because I did. Maybe not out loud, but in the shadows of my pain, I did.

Soon after Amber's funeral I felt a strong pull to get back to my business; my writing. I desperately wanted to get back to the projects that my daughter and I had been talking about and working on. I wanted to move forward with our dreams of empowering the world. My feelings were so intense, as if, somehow, it would make my Amber's life have more meaning.

However, my thoughts and my actions didn't seem to want to work together. Every time I sat at my computer in the dining room, I would find myself wander to the spare room to be close to Amber's things. I felt compelled to read through her journals again and again. Even though I wanted to stay focused on living in the now, I found myself weeping uncontrollably as I held her teddy bear close to my heart.

During those first few weeks, I'd crawl into bed in the middle of the day, emotionally exhausted. I'd wrap myself up in Amber's favourite blanket, which still held her scent. I often cried myself to sleep wishing she was still alive. At times, my emotional pain was so crushing that my heart felt like it didn't have room to beat in my chest. Those beginning days, I'd often take long baths as I sang religious songs of comfort that echoed in the bathroom while I allowed my tears to stream down my cheeks. Doing these things felt strangely liberating while my soul searched for meaning.

Grief involves more than feelings; it can be all consuming. Natural release of pain comes through tears, through crying, through expression. If we do not allow our inner pain to come out, we suppress our spirit. I believe this can weaken us, maybe not physically, but spiritually. What happens when we don't allow our emotions to surface and be released can be deadly to our physical, emotional, and psychological well-being.

Tranquility is not found in the absence of problems, it is found within the ability to rise above them. Look at what you have instead of what you have lost. It is not what the world takes away; it is what you do with what you have been given.

*"**Life's so ironic. It takes sadness to know what happiness is, noise to appreciate silence & absence to value presence.**"*

~ Unknown

Other People's Grief

Often, we have a hard time dealing with the grief of others. We don't know what to do or what to say. We may say things like, *It is what it is…* or *Time to move forward…* or *Don't waste your energy on what can't be changed.*

However, this is not our position when it comes to another person's loss. Our job as a friend, a family member or an acquaintance is to encourage the journey forward; to allow the pain to run its natural course. If we can detach from our own personal discomfort and be sensitive to the sorrow in the moment, we will be more mindful of what to say or what not to say. Everyone grieves differently.

We accept without question our individual biological identifiers, fingerprints, DNA, etc. On the other hand, we frequently overlook our emotional differences. By accepting that no two people grieve the same way with the same intensity or for the same duration, we gain compassion and empathy.

Remaining aware of our emotional differences will help us relax around those who are grieving. We don't need to know what to say, we just need to be sensitive. Through compassion we become more open to ask questions like, *What can I do for you?* or *How can I help?*

If we feel we have the answer for someone else's process, we might insensitively judge the grieving of others; often those we most want to help.

Our emotional responses are formed from our unique past experiences. Everyone copes differently when consumed by a loss. Our attitudes and past experiences influence how we react to what is going on around us. We are also affected by the role and relationship that the person had with the departed, the circumstances surrounding the death and the influence it has on us now.

What happens if we see someone we love disconnect from their anguish, their hurt and their pain? What should we do when we see someone running from their feelings?

Sometimes, instead of judging someone in regards to grief, we decide to try to take on their pain. We want their pain to go away; we want to make things better, like I did with my son in this next example of *The Help That Harms*.

I mistakenly tried to reduce his pain and grief, in regards to the loss of his sister by inadvertently enabling him to avoid his inner pain. In my need to help my son, I supported his need for denial… while I took on the weight of his world.

> *"God, grant me the serenity to accept the things I cannot change, the courage to change the things I can, and the wisdom to know the difference."*
>
> *~ Serenity Prayer*

The Help that Harms

While dealing with my own grief, I watched helplessly as my son Michael shut off his emotions. An impenetrable wall surrounded him. No one was allowed in and his feelings were not allowed out. Outwardly, he appeared to be handling things okay, all things considered, however, as his mom, I knew this was not the case.

He refused to talk about his sister or the accident. People assured me that everyone handles their grief differently; *He'll face his pain when he's ready* is what was said. My heart ached for him. He was only nineteen, 1 ½ years younger than his sister, too young to have to face such a devastating loss.

The following spring, Michael decided he would start a new life; a life away from the memories, a life away from his shattered world. Appearing impulsive, he made plans to meet up with friends in Vancouver, British Columbia, Canada.

 He asked his father, Jeff, and I if we would give our blessing on his decision to move by helping to cover the cost of the flight and some start-up money.
 The money was to tide him over until he found a job. We knew he needed to spread his wings and start his own life, however, we also knew he was dabbling in drugs, a hobby that we did not approve of.
 We hesitantly, but respectfully agreed.
 It was difficult to say goodbye. Nine months earlier, also at an airport, I had said my last goodbye to his sister

Amber.

Through the corner of my eye, I watched Michael impatiently wait. His pants were too big for his tall, thin frame. *I hope that he eats properly.* I thought to myself. I couldn't tell if he was excited, scared, or angry.

His eyes, his gestures, his stance were foreign to me. The young man before me had the focus of a person getting ready to jump out of a plane, not get into one.

It was time.

Michael looked at me as he opened up his arms, inviting me to give him the hug that I yearned to give him. I looked up at him after our quick hug and whispered, "Love you Michael. If you need anything, let me know."

He nodded as he moved into the security line. With a deliberate sense of disconnection, he did not look back. Once he was through security, he turned left toward the hallway and then, in a moment, he was out of sight.

I looked down as tears welled up within me. I took a moment to gain my composure and then looked up and said a little prayer for our son, *bless his journey God, please take care of my boy!*

* * * *

Michael settled into his new environment with only minor setbacks, considering his inexperience. He found an affordable rooming house and a sales job within a few weeks. That job didn't work out; they didn't pay every day. He soon found another job that did. He had only been in training with the second job for a few days when *the call* came in.

"Michael's dead! I mean, my phone is almost dead" his father screamed. "Michael's in the hospital. He's been involved in a fire. We don't know how bad it is. All we know is, he's been taken by ambulance to Vancouver emergency. It's bad! Third degree burns, I don't know anything more I gotta go, my phone's almost dead, I'll call you later!"

The call went dead in my ear as I tried to grasp what I just heard.

The details of what happened that evening were unclear, however, what I have since been told is:

Michael was awakened by the sound and feel of a smouldering fire. The foot of his bed was on fire. He immediately began slapping the sparks that had jumped onto his pants. He grabbed his blanket to suffocate the flames that were climbing angrily up the wall.

Engrossed in these efforts, he was oblivious to the extreme danger that surrounded him. He was more than aware of the danger to the others sleeping in the overcrowded boarding house if he didn't put out the fire.

After extinguishing the fire, he felt an excruciating pain. His hands burned from the heat of the flames. He rushed to the kitchen to run them under some cool running water; however, instead of the relief he expected, his hands throbbed in agony as he watched his skin peel from his raw fingers. His skin hung from his hands like thin tissue paper.

Someone had already called 911. Michael was taken by ambulance to Vancouver Emergency. He had suffered extensive burns to all his fingers, his leg and the bottom of his foot. Strong pain medication was administered at the same time as they treated his injuries.

Michael's Auntie Jackie and Uncle Roland, who live

nearby, were called to pick him up from the hospital the following day. It was clear that he had been through hell. He was emotional and distraught. Michael leaned on his crutches to keep pressure off of the bottom of his raw foot. Thick dressings covered his burns.

Upon discharge he was given a prescription for pain medication and strict instructions to come back every day for dressing changes.

Unbeknownst to Michael, his Dad had jumped on the first available flight to Vancouver. He was determined to bring our son back to Winnipeg where he believed Michael belonged.

The tug of war between father and son was a hellish one. Michael did not want to come back. They both had their own agenda. Somewhere along the line, I became the mediator in the standoff that ensued.

As I spoke on the phone with both of them, my heart was torn. I understood why Michael didn't want to leave Vancouver. He was an adult. He had a right to his own life. On the other hand, I felt badly for Michael's father. He was frustrated with his lack of control over our son's decisions.

I was able to be a buffer between Jeff and Michael through the borage of phone calls I received from them both. I felt helpless.

After two days of deliberations, we had an agreement: I assured Michael that if he did decide to come back to Winnipeg where I could help him, I would personally drive him back to Vancouver after he felt better. He reluctantly agreed...

Upon arrival in Winnipeg, Michael was assisted off the airplane in a wheel chair by a flight attendant. He looked ragged and worn. His eyes revealed immense pain and discomfort. After his disgruntled tales of his painful flight, he said in an agitated tone, "I need a cigarette."

I was confused. I'd never smoked. "Why are you asking me?" I questioned.

He looked over at a woman who was smoking on the sidewalk and said, "Bum a cigarette off that lady." I hurried over to the woman and nervously explained that my son would like a cigarette. She generously gave Michael one and lit it for him.

Michael was in extreme agony but he didn't want to see a doctor until the morning. I understood as it was past midnight.

I took him back to the apartment. As we entered Michael asked me, "Mom, can you help me?"

I quickly responded, "Anything for you Michael, anything."

He looked directly at me and asked sadly, "Can you help me hobble onto the balcony so I can smoke some pot to help with my pain?"

I looked down at my feet. I knew I shouldn't. I knew my boyfriend would be very upset with me. Somehow though, I justified it. "Do you have marijuana on you?" I nervously asked.

"Yes," he said.

The bottom of his foot was severely burnt. He could not put pressure on that leg, so I helped balance him until we were on the balcony. He sat down and rummaged through his things. He anxiously searched for his pipe. He asked in a frustrated tone, "Do you have a drink can?" I quickly ran to the kitchen and emptied a full one.

When I returned, he was fumbling through his back pack. "Can you pull out the lighter? Can you light this on top over here and hold the can at the same time?" he asked in an irritated tone.

I looked at him in disbelief. *I can't believe that he is asking me to do this,* I thought to myself. I looked at him for a moment. He looked so sad and lost. His hands were more like paws because of how they had been bandaged. I once again justified what I was about to do. I had promised I would help.

My hands shook as he impatiently told me that what I was doing was wrong. He was in pain, I reminded myself.

* * * *

Early the next morning, we went to emergency as planned. Michael expected to get his prescription refilled and then be on his way. But that is far from what happened.

The emergency doctor took one look at Michael's injuries and said he would have to be transferred to the Health Science Centre where he would be admitted in the burn ward. He needed skin grafts.

The doctor was baffled that Michael had been released from the Vancouver hospital and that he had even been allowed on a plane in his severe condition.

Michael looked at me as if I had betrayed him, "You said we were just coming in to get a new prescription for pain killers and then we could go!" he whimpered.

I began to cry as I tried to explain, "No Michael, I said I would help you get better; the doctors know best."

Michael moaned for more pain relief as he laid

waiting on the stretcher. The nurses repeatedly explained that they had to wait until he was transferred to the next hospital before he could be given more painkillers. I paced the corridor as if it would somehow speed up the process.

Michael was taken by ambulance to the Health Science Centre. Upon arrival, he was given more medication and they began removing the dead skin from his wounds. This painful procedure would have to be endured every day thereafter.

Later that afternoon, Michael pleaded with me to ask the doctors or nurses to increase his pain medication. He felt the pain killers weren't giving him any relief. I whispered to him, "Michael, please tell your doctor of any other drugs you may have been using."

He flatly refused.

On the second day Michael agreed that I could allude to his recreational drug use. I approached the head nurse and asked, "Can you let the doctor know Michael may have been doing street drugs? I'm afraid his system needs more pain killers because of his possible tolerance."

The head nurse looked at me and sternly replied, "Look Mom. I know you care about your son, but he's an adult. If he has been taking things, he needs to tell us. Then, and only then, can we increase his medication."

I understood what she was saying but, I needed to finish my plea, "I think he's afraid to tell you guys. He thinks he will be in trouble." I replayed his excuse, or should I say my rationalisation for him. I begged on behalf of Michael as I tried to hold back my emotions, "He's been running from himself since his sister passed away less than a year ago. Please help him."

The nurse looked at me and said, "You have an

incredibly smart young man in that hospital bed. Maybe it's time you let him take care of him. You've done your job, Mom. Now it's time for him to take control of his life."

I knew what she was saying. I also knew that she was right, but that didn't stop the anguish I felt for my son.

This was indeed an *Aha!* moment for me. I didn't recognize it fully at the time. Maybe because I didn't want to hear her words of wisdom, I just wanted her to make my son's suffering disappear. Nevertheless, the more I replayed her words, the more I could see that I was part of the problem.

As long as we enable our adult children, they can continue to deny, or they may not even be aware that they have a problem since most of their problems are being fixed by those around them. Only when our adult children are forced to face the consequences of their own actions, their choices, and their behaviours, will they see their own weaknesses. If we continue to take care of their problems and issues, self-inflicted or not, *they* don't have a problem: *We* do!

As parents it is difficult to let go of our adult children. Part of the reasons may stem from the, *Would've, Could've, Should'ves* that replay within our mind. However, this is not good for anyone.

If we don't deal with our guilt, we will spend the rest of our lives picking up the pieces for our grown children: Emotionally, financially, or otherwise, in so doing, debilitating them.

As parents we need to separate ourselves from our children's problems without separating from them. When we do this we become a positive force in their lives while getting on with our own lives. This also includes other adults in our lives: Parents, siblings, friends, co-workers and even strangers. We can be supportive but we should not take on other people's issues. When we do, we weaken them, not strengthen them.

"*Sometimes the questions are complicated and the answers are simple.*"

~ Dr. Seuss

Letting Go

After five agonizing days, Michael was finally discharged from the hospital with strict instructions to come back every other day to have his dressings changed.

Moments after leaving the hospital, Michael looked at me and said, "Ok, I'm ready to go back to Vancouver!"

I stared at him in disbelief. There he stood, his hands wrapped up like a mummy, clumsily leaning against the crutches that protected his bound foot. After a moment of processing what he wanted, I nodded in agreement as I tried to figure out the details of the trip.

I wasn't going to argue with him. "Yes Michael, I told you I would bring you back when you were ready," I said, "Are you ready?"

He nodded an emphatic yes.

"Well then," I reluctantly agreed, "We will leave tomorrow morning. I will bring you to Vancouver with my blessing. But, like I said to you earlier, I will no longer be financing you besides your first month rent."

Michael sharply acknowledged, "I know! You said that already. I know what I'm doing!"

* * * *

We began our trip the next morning as planned. My boyfriend wanted to come along. We rented a larger car so that Michael had room to stretch his legs out for the long road trip before us.

After driving with only one short hotel break, we arrived safely in Vancouver 32 hours later. Our first stop was the hospital. Michael went straight in to have his dressings changed as we waited.

Before we left Winnipeg, Michael had arranged a place to rent in Vancouver with a different batch of friends; he had metaphorically and physically burned a bridge with the last place. During our drive, he had been trying to call his friends to confirm our arrival time, but there had been no answer.

After Michael was finished at the hospital, we went to a Wal-Mart to pick up a few basics for his new beginning. It is here that he connected with his future roommates through texts.

The reason that his two friends had not responded to him earlier was that, unbelievably, they had just been released from the hospital themselves. They had both been hit by a drunk driver while they were walking at a crosswalk the day before. As a mother I was thinking, *I couldn't write this type of crazy!*

We soon arrived at the house. I saw no door to the front entrance. I looked at the young man through the doorway. He was obviously still wearing the clothes from his last night's horror. His head was swollen. He held a beer can up to Michael when he saw him as he proudly bellowed, "Topping up the old painkillers." The young woman beside him didn't look like she was in as bad shape, although she had obvious road rash with dried blood spots on her jeans.

The moment we stopped the car, it was obvious Michael wanted *Mom* gone. I quickly helped him unload his stuff. It was time to say goodbye once again.

I gave him an uncomfortable hug as I whispered, "Good luck Michael. If you need anything, besides money, let me know. I believe in you. I love you!"

I quickly went to the car.

As we drove away, tears streamed down my cheeks.

I felt an overwhelming amount of love for my son. He was old enough to make his own choices, right or wrong. I had to let go.

After arriving home in Winnipeg, I felt an overpowering urge to write Michael a letter of encouragement. I wanted him to know that I believed in him. Yes, I didn't like the situation he was in, but I wanted him to know how I felt.

After I finished writing the letter, I felt a freedom that comes from releasing false control. I ended the letter with a declaration to Michael and to myself.

Below are the words I wrote to him. It reflects my feelings within it.

Dear Michael,

We all encounter struggles through the journey of life. Narrow paths congested by debris, long winding roads hidden within gloomy fog; deep valleys of compressed darkness where the light of day is no longer visible.

Do not allow these times to dampen your spirit. The bright meadows of golden blossoms will be revealed. The soothing sound of nature's beauty is patiently waiting.

Through it all, the only constant is the core of Truth within you. If you follow your Truth as your compass; if you allow your heart to guide you, you will fulfill your destiny. On the other hand, if you follow someone else's path, you will feel lost because the path that you have chosen is not yours. When you walk away from your Truth you lose touch with your spirit, your inner guide. If this happens, stop right where you are, become very still. Reach within you to find your spirit again, return to your inner voice, otherwise, you will simply go around in circles, becoming more lost.

You are everything you need to be, just as you are, right now. You are the center of your own life. This is all a part of life. As you walk your path, other people will join you for a time: a friend, a lover, a spouse, a parent and even a child. Not all people are meant to remain in your life. Some of these people who have shared in your journey will have been for but a time.

Be glad when others walk beside you, enjoy their company, connect as closely and deeply as you can, but always, always, shine your own light and walk your own path and allow them to do the same.

From this Day forward

I will allow my life to flow and evolve
I will accept others for who they are.
I will have the courage to follow my heart.
I will embrace my uniqueness.
I will stand up for my convictions.
I will not control or manipulate others.
I will allow others to own their world, as I will own mine.

Thank you for teaching me how to let go Michael

Love Mom

One of the many things that I have learned through this life experience was: True love is letting go of control. Truth is, we have no more control over others than we have over the wind in the air.

The only real change we can make is from within. How we react and what we do with the circumstances we face are the only ways we can affect change.

Growth is fundamentally the willingness to let go; letting go of the illusion of control. When we give up control, we gain it. When we let go of our judgements, we allow life to reveal itself in its wholeness. By doing this, we become free to see the variety of possibilities. We can then flow more easily from black to white, inside to outside, wrong to right, failure to success.

Everything has an opposite. If we want to experience a full, rich life, we need to view both sides without preconceptions. We cannot have one without the other. Our thoughts, feelings, and actions cannot remain in conflict if we are to have peace.

True peace is found through the alignment of our inner and outer world. We cannot be fully accepted by ourselves or others if we reject any part of who we are.

Acknowledge what is, who you are, where you are, your frailties, your weaknesses, and your strengths. No judgment, just acceptance. Every solution has a problem.

Acceptance of other people and conditions is really saying

yes to what is. In essence, acceptance is an alignment with Truth. However, what if you are not aligned with Truth? What if you are operating with an improper perception? What if what you think is Truth is far from it?

"There are things known and there are things unknown, and in between are the doors of perception."

~ Aldous Huxley

Reality vs. Perception

There are many ways to not live in reality. One of the most common ways is through denial; our natural defence mechanism. When a person is faced with a Truth which is too difficult to accept and they reject it despite overwhelming evidence, denial is in play.

Everyone's Truth is different due to view points and opinions. It is through our perceptions that we evaluate our experiences. It is our opinions, thoughts, and emotions that create our perceptions, shaping our experiences. This gets more complicated because our perceptions are influenced by our past experiences, our beliefs and expectations. This is part of the reason why everyone's perceptions of reality are different.

Challenging our perceptions, good or bad, is essential if we are to move forward. Then, and only then, can we take our individual challenges to the next level; deliberately unlocking and dissecting the hidden treasures found within our lessons.

When we are secure enough in ourselves to question our version of the Truth, we can change the way we see the world around us, thus changing our world.

Today, right now, this minute, you have the ability to repair the perspective of whatever happened yesterday and re-direct the course of tomorrow. Yes, the past is important because this is the place where all your resources, learning and life lessons have come from. However, it is not a place to linger. So, why then are so many people stuck in the past? Why are their thoughts anchored to moments that they, for whatever reason, cannot or will not let go of? Why do so many people feel the need to live in a place that no longer exists?

In order to answer these questions, we must first understand how our memory works. Studies have shown that we do not remember things exactly the way they were. Every time we remember something, we are, in essence, recreating it in our mind.

Memories are formed from our recollection of the bits and pieces of actions, behaviours, people, and emotions that were most notable within those moments and stored in a sort of mental cabinet. In order to gain access to our memories, we have to pull a stored *emotion* off of one shelf, a *behaviour* from another shelf, an *action* from a third shelf, and so on and so on.

When we form our memories, adopt an attitude, or create our opinions, we do so based upon our *perception* of reality, not on reality itself.

Deep down, I believe, we all consider our perception of ourselves, and the world around us, to be fairly accurate. Yes, we know that we can't comprehend everything, so we make the necessary mental adjustments to help us understand the world around us. This creates stability in our emotional foundation for us to build on. This is logical, however, what if we have built our lives on false concepts?

It is the purpose of this book to re-acquaint you with your world, your mind, and your spirit. In order to do this, it is important to refrain from any preconceived judgements about success and failure. This may sound difficult, but it is necessary.

When we label people or things we no longer see them in their fullness. What we judge, we cannot understand. The only difference between a weed and a flower is our perception.

Through acceptance, we gain access to the profound process of life's ever-changing moments. With this, our experiences of failure or success can be re-framed and understood as a necessary, meaningful process.

"If you put yourself in a position where you have to stretch outside your comfort zone, then you are forced to expand your consciousness."

~ Les Brown

Avoiding Emotions

When we run from our emotions, we complicate our experiences. Everyone does it sometimes, and some do it regularly. Avoidance behaviour is self-sabotaging because when we attempt to fix a problem by avoiding it or by adding a new problem to it (one that does not deal with the initial problem), we perpetuate the problem.

Self-medicating with food, drugs, alcohol, shopping and/or gaming are all common forms of avoidance. Procrastination is another way of side-stepping our negative feelings. The more extreme avoidance strategies result in self-injury. We all do this at times to escape our painful feelings. The problem lies within the avoidance. Avoiding emotions can sabotage your dreams. Is it possible that you are sabotaging yourself?

Self-sabotage is not an act, it's a process; a complex, sad process that temporarily distracts us from our overwhelming feelings. Because the effects of our negative behaviour may not show up for some time, we aren't always aware that we are doing this.

Addicts, for example, have a range of excuses and justifications as to why they avoid *whatever it is* that they are running from, often not knowing the real issue of *what* they are running from.

The problem with any type of avoidance is, more often than not, that it adds insult to injury. Hiding or running from a negative emotion generally adds more problems to the initial issue, creating more problems.

Everyday our strength of character is tested. The pressure of life, the conflicts and the chaos all test the determination of our dreams. What if we have lost touch with our initial heart's purpose due to the distractions of our less than focused life?

Distraction through self-inflicted chaos has many possible reasons. I know, because I have found myself in the middle of it more than I care to admit. In fact, I am writing this because I had again found myself guilty of subconsciously sabotaging my ultimate vision; my image of success!

Throughout my colourful life, I've become more than comfortable with failure. I've trained myself to recognize and accept my shortcomings and weaknesses and then build upon them. Like a moth to a flame, I felt drawn toward my challenges. My life has taught me the importance of learning and growing through the failure process.

Every failure has held a unique lesson within it. From these experiences, I've learned to recognize the warning signs while remaining objective. Somewhere along the line, I lost track of what I was doing. I had become more focused on my distractions than the quest I had set out to accomplish.

We are survivors by nature. We focus first on things that need our attention. We take care of our immediate needs, and then... we move in the direction of our growth.

Is it possible that you are sabotaging your dreams? What if you are off-track but you don't know it? What if your chaos has flipped you upside down? What if you've become *reactive* rather than *proactive*? What if, somewhere along the line, you have stopped moving toward your goals?

As I pull together the last part of this book *Beyond Failure* I have become aware of my now obvious, self-inflicted chaos. Allow me to elaborate...

Less than a year after Amber's death, I said goodbye to my boyfriend, of a year-and-a-half. I packed up my things and moved into a broken-down house that I purchased, about ½ hour drive south of Winnipeg, in Morris, Manitoba.

My thoughts regarding the sad abandoned house (which I lovingly called "the cabin") was that I would fix it up while living in it. Once the renovations were done, I would sell it for a profit.

I saw the cabin as an opportunity and a solution to many of my troubles and problems. Although, in all fairness, I didn't calculate the extent of the difficulties the cabin would add to my already hectic world.

My thinking was; when I wasn't running my business, writing, speaking, arranging seminars, managing a non-profit organization, creating videos and inspiring others, I could tear down a few walls and dig out the basement in my spare time.

I envisioned I would still have more than enough time for the important things in life like being a reliable and loving mom, sister, daughter and friend. Somehow, this investment, with its extra workload, strangely made sense to me.

Beyond Failure

Part of my vision for my fixer-upper was to hire my son to work with me. We would magically bring the old two story house back from the brink of ruin.

Michael and I would joyfully work together as we built an unbreakable Mother/ Son bond through the transformational process. Michael's youthful energy combined with my experience and expertise would restore the cabin to better than original condition (If I could insert a musical tune here it would be ...whistle while you work...do, da... do... do... do do...do).

My ultimate vision for the project was that while working through the extreme renovations, my son would see that with enough determination, things that once appeared hopeless could be conquered.

Bonus points: One of the walls in the basement had started to bow-in and needed reinforcement. This is where you might question my sanity concerning the undertaking of this project. On the contrary, I fell in love with the metaphorical significance of this challenging issue; an actual visual of what happens to a structure when it is built upon a weak foundation.

Our mind, body and soul would be transformed through this project.

Can I hear an AMEN?

Okay, okay... admittedly a fixer upper house is not the easiest environment to live in, but I knew that. I had successfully flipped three houses prior to this old house while Amber and Michael were growing up.

I wasn't worried about my developing business either. I was more than familiar with this world. Juggling multiple projects, objectives and deadlines is where I thrived.

All the businesses I had operated, bought and sold had been subsidized by my property investments and/or side jobs. This was how I kept my dreams alive.

I moved forward with my vision into my new-old fixer-upper house September 1st, my son following soon after. We began the projects as planned, but as we all know... plans change.

In the Eye of the Storm

On occasion, it's nice to escape reality through our daydreams, envisioning what we wish our lives looked like rather than what reality reveals. Sometimes due to the frailty of our mind or the depth of our pain, we lose touch with life and slip into a false reality, either ours or someone else's. This happens most often because, for whatever reason, we find it too difficult to face the harsh sting of reality.

Tears streamed down my cheeks as I tried desperately to scrub away the painful words painted on the wall before me: Murder! Suck rats in Hell! The dripping accusation, like the moment, refused to wash away. Immersed in a nightmare, my thoughts of normalcy lay broken and scattered around me. What happened? I must wake up...this can't be real!

Hours earlier, life had been normal. What or who brought me to this horrifying reality or more importantly, what was reality?

* * * *

It started off as a cool November, Sunday afternoon. I had left my 20 year old son, Michael, at home for the weekend while I enjoyed an overnight shopping getaway with a friend to Grand Forks, a neighboring US border city.

Upon arriving home, I gathered up my purchases from my friend's car which we had taken on the trip. With my arms filled to capacity with shopping bags, I managed to wave a big thank-you and turned towards the house. Balancing the bags in my hands, I wiggled through the porch door.

As I entered, an unusual draft blew from inside the house. The porch was cold and dark. The heavy entrance door to the house was partly open. The window that had been in the door was shattered. Jagged shards precariously hung along the edge of the window frame. My eyes were drawn to the floor as I felt the crunch of broken glass beneath my feet. Time slowed as my reality shifted.

In the half-light I could see partway inside the house. The floor to the entrance was covered with broken pieces of familiar remains. A Rubbermaid container, overflowing with a mix of irrational contents blocked the entrance. I carefully pushed the door open as the door shoved the large items out of the way. I stepped inside. A chill came over me. Something was very wrong.

Beyond the door, everything in the entrance-way lay broken and scattered. *What happened?* I thought to myself. It was as if a hurricane had ripped through my home. My concerns quickly turned to my son, *where's Michael?*

Stepping over various foreign items, I turned towards the living room and immediately had my answer. There before me, my 6'1" son was standing shaking like a leaf. A look of horror blanketed his face as he screamed, "Why did you do it?"

In confusion, I moved toward him. His voice was hoarse and strained as he started screaming louder in short, biting accusations, "Why did you kill her?" His body shook uncontrollably; his eyes shot out forceful streams of hysterical rage, "I know what you did! I KNOW what you did!"

Speechless, I searched for meaning, *what happened? What's happening?* I wondered. Unable to piece together what I was seeing or what he was talking about, I continued moving forward.

My maternal instincts moved me toward Michael. I needed to calm him. I wanted to hold him in that instant; protect him and let him know everything was going to be okay. Just inches from reaching him, his anger escalated as though I was his enemy.

Intuitively, I swerved past him as if on autopilot. The level of destruction around me was mind-numbing. *What is he saying? What has happened here?*

As my eyes adjusted to the shadows, it appeared everything within my scope of vision was destroyed. The bookshelves were tossed across the living room, laying twisted upon the floor, their contents strewn from one end of the room to the other. Bits and pieces of my world lay broken and destroyed around me.

In a daze, I continued moving forward. As I entered the kitchen, a cold wind blew directly onto my face. On the far wall, one of the glass panes in the window appeared to have exploded, allowing the harsh winter breeze to enter. Fragments of shattered glass lay frozen across the countertop. Above me, all four fan blades of the light fixture were bent bizarrely downward. Beside me, the kitchen sink water faucet had been forcibly bent upwards. Water spewed erratically through the cracks in the distended metal, pooling onto the floor.

In shock, I turned around, intending to go back to my son. However, what I saw next stopped me in my tracks.

Before me, a long handled scythe impaled my fridge, the blade eerily plunged in the middle of the fridge door. The handle stuck out, suspended motionless in the air. The deep gashes beside the blade revealed that it was the third stabbing attempt that finally stuck.

I started to shake as I became more aware that I couldn't deal with this situation on my own. I was in danger! My son was in danger! I needed to get back to the front door as that was the only logical way out.

As I re-entered the living room, I nervously passed my son who had not moved from his position. He was now screaming louder, "Murderer! WHY? Why did you kill her?"

"I'm going to get help," I stammered, as I tried to hide my fear.

His outrage intensified, "Show me! You killed her!"

With a shake in my voice, I again assured him, "I'm going to get help." I backed slowly out the front door, all the while maintaining eye contact with my son.

In grateful disbelief, I saw that my friend hadn't left yet. He was just pulling out of the driveway. I waved my arms franticly. *I need help! Please don't leave* my gestures pleaded.

* * * *

It was not difficult to talk Michael into going to sit in the car with my friend because, from my son's standpoint, I was the enemy. I watched from the corner of the window as they talked. I had initially tried to stand outside to show my son I was worried about him, but he became even more agitated, screaming like a caged animal, "I know what you did, you killed her!"

My head was spinning. The chill in the air, the darkness of the house cruelly magnified the hell that engulfed us. I watched in suspended silence as my son talked animatedly in the car. After only a few moments, my friend came in to tell me that he would take my son to the hospital. I watched in utter helplessness as they drove away.

Words alone cannot describe the emotions that flooded through me as my world lay smashed and broken around me. Fragments of who I thought I was were scattered amid the ruins.

It is here, in the stillness, that I saw the carnage of my undoing. It is here that I was forced to confront my harsh reality. It is here that I came face to face with my fears. The emotions I was desperately trying to subdue were overpowering. It is here, in my brokenness that I gave up my illusion of control.

My desire had been to be the best Mom to my children but I had failed. I dreamed of sharing my limitless visions of possibilities to help change the world…but I had failed! Within the shadows of my destruction, I gave up control….

It was within this darkness that I learned my greatest lesson…

"When you are down on your back, if you can look up, you can get up."

~ *Les Brown*

Illusions

When it comes to other people's lives, we have no more control over them than we have over the wind in the air or the waves in the ocean. When our focus is on changing others, we detach from our personal responsibilities. This sets us up for failure because we believe that people and circumstances should be in a specifically set way.

No matter how carefully we plan our life, things will not always go as planned. Things are rarely as simple as they appear. If we are not careful, not only can we get sucked into an illusion that seems real, but we begin to believe the greatest illusion of them all: The illusion of control.

We all struggle with control at some level. This is often because we are afraid that we won't be able to handle the ups and downs of life. Is it fear that creates the need to try to control what others think about us? Are we afraid that we won't be accepted?

We make life more difficult when we do not let go of what we cannot control.

We must let go of the illusion of control.

When something we believe is in question, we are given an incredible opportunity for growth. In these moments, we are forced to question our reality. It is within these interruptions that we are given a glimpse into our intangible inner world. When our world is flipped upside down, for whatever reason, we cannot help but see a totally different perspective. As a result, we have access to a deeper knowledge that we would not have had from our sheltered, opinionated viewpoint.

Within the darkness of our unknowing, the light of Truth, a non-physical, divine light can be seen. Through this shift in consciousness, a higher dimension of reality becomes visible. It is here that we are given a flash of clarity. These moments are often referred to as *an awakening*.

Change always provides an opportunity for growth. Often we are not open to change, therefore we do not grow. When we are too focused on keeping things a certain way, we fight *what is*.

When we let go of our illusions, we are left with Truth, our core, our authentic self, our spirit. When we connect to our spirit, we disconnect from our judgements of what should be. Change will happen whether we accept it or not. So why not accept it?

> **"There is nothing either good or bad but thinking makes it so."**
>
> *~ William Shakespeare*

Within the Darkness

When we let go of our need to control, we gain freedom. When we allow things that we have no control over to happen, accepting that everything is as it is, we gain peace, the kind of peace that passes all understanding, knowing that there is a higher purpose within the transformational moment. This brings healing.

As the dust settled, my mind and my body did not want to align with the carnage that surrounded me. Disconnected from my world, I searched for meaning… but there was none. Pacing the floor, I picked up some of the remnants of what I used to value. *What happened?* My home, my life and my world lay shattered before me.

Some of the floorboards upstairs had been torn out of place; a bedroom door on the main floor had been ripped off its hinges. It now lay strangely out of place in the middle of the floor in an upstairs bedroom.

Searching for answers, I walked toward the basement. A bizarre mix of coffee grounds and barbeque sauce led the way down the unstable stairs. At the base of the stairwell lay portions of my coffee machine and coffee grinder. Pieces of broken glass and plastic scattered in every direction.

As I entered the basement, I stared into the shadowed chaos. Twisted metal was scattered on the cement floor. I looked toward the gas furnace that now squeaked unnaturally. I could see the fan belt winding around the motor. I realized in that moment that the metal sheets that lay crumpled on the floor were the exhaust ducts that had been attached to the furnace. *Oh my, this is not good*, I thought to myself as I franticly ran back up the stairs to shut the thermostat off. I had no idea of the possible danger of this type of situation

My hands were shaking as I picked up my phone, I needed help. After only a few rings my twin brother Richard answered. I tried to sound as calm as I could as I explained what was happening and expressed my concern about my safety. He assured me that I had done the right thing by turning everything off and would come over right away. As I hung up the phone, I felt some relief.

My thoughts kept returning to my son and the indescribable hell he must have experienced over the past 24 hours as the displaced contents of my house revealed. He had been through so much in his short life. *Why did he have to go through this?*

A shroud of incomprehensible darkness filled the house. I continued picking up the remnants of what used to be. I paced through the chaos trying to piece together what happened. In my hand I held a wooden statue of a duck that once had a head. It was all so much to have to deal with.

I had a vision for my life, but this was not it. The dreams I held refused to materialize outside of me. I had fought to be strong, but I was weak. My vision was to rise above my circumstances, to be an example of possibilities but I failed.

The world that I found myself in clashed with everything in me. My idealistic concepts of life were nowhere to be found. In my brokenness, I could see that I was nothing. Within the darkness of my humility, I let go. I didn't care about what anyone thought or felt about me. I didn't have the answers.

Within the shadows, I looked up to heaven and cried. "I am not this strong, I am weak. I am broken. I am nothing. Please help me!" I sobbed. "I release to you my son, I let go. This is not my son's fault. Please be with him. I have made so many mistakes, take me instead. I beg of you, please, please save my son from the hell he has entered."

As my tears flowed in the stillness, I felt an extraordinary release. An unexplainable calm came over me. My perception of who I thought I was transformed into a greater awareness of who I was. In the shadows of my despair I felt a shift in my consciousness. The warmth that permeated my being was familiar and comforting. An indescribable peace, a peace that passed understanding permeated my soul.

The message I knew in that moment was...

All is as it should be. Do not fight what is not yours to fight. His life is not yours, and your life is not his. You cannot give something that you do not possess. You can do nothing for another that you have not done for yourself. Be still and know. You and everything around you are perfectly imperfect. Continue to move forward. Keep on growing and learning, for you will never know everything. Persist in what is in your heart. Stay open to what you are still to learn. It is your intention that will move you forward. Grow in peace and love...For that is the essence of every soul.

In the silence, I felt my spirit blend with everything around me. Everything was part of a harmonious creation of change. All was connected in a universal balance. The world was perfectly imperfect.

What we have and who we believe we are, are only a construct of our minds. I felt relaxed in this knowing. It felt natural even though nothing I was experiencing was in any way *normal*.

The disorder that surrounded me was only a surface reflection of a deeper collective pain, a universal convergence. I felt a detachment from the outside world like it was not a part of me. On the other hand, a reconciliation of everything that was around me formed my completeness. My concept of individuality was gone as I felt the wholeness of our collective unity.

My belief system shifted. I could see that my feelings were just my perspective; my beliefs. I could see that my desire to change others was ineffective.

My impulse to fix what was broken dissipated in my knowing. Nothing is truly broken. Allow people to be what they are. Allow them to evolve and transcend the issues that they need to face on their journey. Appreciate and value everyone; where they are, as they are, and who they are. No one is greater than another.

What I took from this experience was worth the encounter I had with darkness; for the light that was revealed. We were able to get help; help I had been unaware that we needed. In fact, this experience turned out to be one of the biggest blessings in disguise.

I'm excited to see how my son will speak to those who are waiting for his unique insight, for he, too, has a depth of understanding that only comes from the perspective of brokenness.

Pain is unavoidable, but suffering is not. How we respond to pain is within our own control. People who have experienced deep suffering know this because there is a breaking point. When this happens, surrender becomes unavoidable. Suffering turns into stillness.

Within your deepest pain and disappointments, within the darkness of your sorrow, lies an opportunity for an awakening. These moments have transformational abilities. When life reveals that you are not the centre of your exterior environment, you are forced to go within. It is here in the stillness, that you can become aware of your spirit, your Truth.

When we give up the illusion of control over the things around us, we gain an understanding into what we have control over. We are not the centre of the universe. However, we are the centre of *our* universe. When we take full responsibility for ourselves, we become free to grow; free to move towards our personal destiny. When we let go, we no longer need to blame others or our environment because we take ownership of who we are. In our brokenness, we are left bare and transparent.

Your Truth that yearns to be revealed becomes free when you let go of your illusions. Life can continue to reflect the disharmony and chaos that our evolving universe is a part of, but it no longer has to affect your internal world. Yes, you will still experience pain, but without the unnecessary suffering.

When you stop running from what is you, give yourself the

opportunity to appreciate the meaning within the moment instead of wasting your energy trying to control what you have no control over. You become open to everything that enters your life; open to learn, open to change and open to grow.

When you let go of your illusions, your spirit will rise forth triumphantly to greet a reality that is always acceptable. You will be at peace as you move forward in eager anticipation of what Truth will reveal. Believe in yourself.

Don't fight what is. Acknowledge it. Thank it. Grow from it! We come to this world of success by passing through the land of failure. Success is born in solitude and stillness. Even during our darkest times, we are not without hope because we are here. We are alive.

"Things seen are temporal and things unseen are eternal."

~ Helen Keller

Acceptance

Through acceptance, you will realize that you have been guided to this infinite desert. In the beginning it will seem lonely and scary because you are not used to it. What you have fought to avoid, you now face.

Here is where you will see the reality about your thoughts, your actions, and your fears. Here is where you will discover how some of your concepts about failures and successes have been wrong. It is here that you will find what you have been seeking.

During this transformational time, the desert begins to blossom. You will see what you were previously unable to see; life within death, success within failure.

Transitions can provide opportunities for stretching our comfort zone, facilitating growth. During these times, new opportunities introduce themselves. Let us embrace and welcome them. Let us let go of our illusions.

I no longer dream of changing the world. I now focus on changing myself. In spite of my ignorance, life has taught me that people will not change what they do not want to change. Our lives are about us; about our personal transformation and about our personal healing.

The question then becomes, how do we change?

The words that are written on the tomb of Anglo-Saxon Bishop (1100 A.D.) in the crypts of Westminster Abbey reflect the wisdom of acceptance: Below is a representation of those words.

Anglo-Saxon Bishop
1100 A.D.

When I was young and free my imagination had no limits, I dreamed of changing the world.

As I grew older and wiser, I discovered the world would not change, so I shortened my sights somewhat and decided to change only my country. But it, too, seemed immovable.

As I grew into my twilight years, in one last desperate attempt, I settled for changing only my family, those closest to me, but alas, they would have none of it.

And now, as I lie on my deathbed, I suddenly realize: If I had only changed myself first, then by example I would have changed my family. From their inspiration and encouragement, I would then have been able to better my country, and who knows, I may have even changed the world.

Awareness

The path of change involves awareness, acceptance, and action. Through my process of self-change, I inadvertently stumbled upon a fundamental Truth: We need to be aware of being unaware.

It is natural to seek approval from our friends, family, and sometimes even strangers to justify our thoughts and behaviours. We love to hear, "It's not your fault, keep on doing what you're doing." By hearing affirmations, we can continue to justify our actions. If we are faced with disapproval, we may become even more stubborn in our resolve and think, *I'll show them, what do they know?*

It appears that we are more concerned with changing other people's opinions rather than changing ourselves. The secret to change is being open. Change is not found in others. It is found within ourselves.

Being aware... of being unaware... helps us to stay aware!

With awareness we become more open to possibilities that we may otherwise not see. Being aware that life is not always going to go as planned is a big step. No matter how hard we try, we'll never be able to completely control our surroundings.

One thing that we can all count on is the certainty that life will be filled with consistent inconsistencies; and this will never change. With awareness and acceptance of what brought you to this point, you become free from negative judgments, thereby appreciating how your journey has shaped you and transformed you for the better.

Setbacks need to be expected, accepted, and even embraced. Embracing obstacles sounds ridiculous, however, seeing as they are unavoidable, but why not? By remaining aware of the probability of unforeseen problems, we gain the advantage of anticipating the unexpected, thus becoming prepared. We can then embrace what is behind us and what is before us.

Life is a struggle. Anyone who says otherwise has not yet lived. Throughout our journey, we will have curveballs thrown at us that may knock the wind out of us. If we allow life to teach us through some of our more humbling struggles, we will grow.

The reason most people never achieve their dreams is because they simply give up. The journey was never meant to be easy. The times when it is most important to endure are the times that you will be most tested.

Another way to look at it is: An up cannot have significance without a down or a wrong without a right. Problems fill our days with variation. Life would not be an adventure if we only had up moments.

"What you resist not only persists, but will grow in size."

~ Carl Gustav Jung

Root Cause

When we identify the root of an issue, we gain the knowledge of how to deal with that problem. Once the root cause is removed from a recurring cycle, the undesirable action will have no reason to continue. Let's dig into a few possible reasons why I seemed to be sabotaging my own success.

Some of the reasons I might have complicated my life could have been that I either knew too much or maybe I needed failure, because within the chaos I found solace. Let's address the first possibility: *I knew too much.* This possibility seems to be illogical on the surface, however, most of us have been hit between the eyes by a simple solution concerning an apparent problem. This is where we ask the obvious questions: *Why didn't I think of the answer earlier?* and, *What was I thinking?*

To understand the *I knew too much* hypothesis, I'm going to change the last question from *what was I thinking?* To, *Why was I over-thinking?* I don't know if that's what I was doing, however, I do know that I had overcomplicated things. I was delaying my success by digging deeper into more projects, ones I didn't need to be doing. I had become too comfortable while distracted within my challenges and problems.

It is natural to overlook the obvious. We often ignore simple solutions in lieu of complicated theories. When we intellectualize, we slow down our progress and occasionally miss our goals.

What often happens when we become too comfortable within our environment, good or bad is that we tend to stay in those familiar surroundings. We do this by creating habits that reinforce our behaviour. Maybe I had inadvertently created a habit of over-thinking and over-analysing; or maybe that's what I'm doing now.

Keeping it simple requires confidence and humility. If we can resolve within ourselves that we don't have to be all-knowing, we would benefit greatly. There's brilliance in simplicity.

Many difficult problems have been solved with the simplest solutions. It's humbling to face our ignorance when we see how an issue could have been avoided or simplified.

Returning to the possibility that I needed failure to reaffirm my life and my existence, when I look back at my chaos, it appears that I was challenging failure. *Come on failure, try to get me! Come out, come out, wherever you are. I double dog dare you!* Is it possible that I needed failure to surround me?

I was not intimidated by failure but maybe it was my security blanket. Maybe I was more comfortable in the middle of chaos than I was in the solace of success. Maybe, subconsciously, I didn't feel worthy of more than what I was creating. Is it possible that you, too, may be sabotaging your own success?

As you reflect upon your actions and accept yourself with all of your shortcomings, you will find freedom. Through reflection, you can see and take full ownership of your mistakes. You cannot break bad habits or stop making the same mistakes if you do not see them. You are your best teacher yet your worst student.

Reflection is a wonderful tool to use in order to look back at a situation and learn from it. Examine the mistake, look at the alternatives that could have been taken, and resolve to do better next time. Continually evaluate. Are you moving forwards or backwards?

"Life is really simple, but we insist on making it complicated."

~ Confucius

Dream

A dream is not an object or a goal; it is the image of possibilities. Dreams do not die; they live on through hardship and defeat. Imagining a better tomorrow starts with a dream. As we imagine the future, we can dream of a better tomorrow, a better self, recognizing the special gifts and talents that we contribute. We are worthy of greatness and our dreams should reflect that.

The majority of us seem to prefer to play it safe rather than take the necessary risks to live out our dreams. Taking risks means the possibility of failure.

Many of us prefer convenience over challenges. The stability of the status quo is not vulnerable to failure. Due to the overwhelming fear of failure, we remain comfortable in our mediocrity.

Build the strength and self-confidence which is necessary to face the ridicule, laughter and negative responses that you will face in the quest of your dreams. The passion within you will ignite the fire of desire and create vision which will help you to reach your dreams.

Those of us who are willing to make the rock-hard decision to take the risks of moving forward and to endure the unavoidable setbacks along the way in pursuit of our purpose, end up living a full rich life.

You can't change a lifetime of who you are in a few weeks

or even months. The transition from mindlessly existing to purposeful living is a difficult and challenging process. Purposeful living will profoundly impact your life in incredible ways. Stay focused on your journey.

Not easy… but well worth it!

Your goals and dreams will develop and transform over a lifetime. Regarding failure as being necessary is critical in your development. Persist in the pursuit of your dreams despite the obstacles that will certainly stand in your way.

As you advance down the road to your dreams, you will definitely fail. Get up, dust yourself off, and continue on to an attainable dream: Your own dream!

"To accomplish great things, we must not only act, but also dream; not only plan, but also believe."

~ Anatole France

Dare to Dream

*"Some people only look at life through
eyes that seldom gleam
while others look beyond today
as they're guided by a dream*

*And the dreamers can't be sidetracked by dissenters
who may laugh for only they alone can know
how special is their path*

*But dreams aren't captured easily;
there's much work before you're through
but the time and efforts are all worthwhile
when the impossible comes true*

*And dreams have strength in numbers
for when a common goal is shared
the once impossible comes true because of all who cared*

*And once it's seen as reality a dream has just begun
for magically from dreams come dreams
And a walk becomes a run*

*But with growth of course comes obstacles
and with obstacles comes fear
but the dream that is worth dreaming
finds its way to the dear*

*And the dream continues growing
Reaching heights before unseen and
it's all because of the courage of the dreamers
and their dream."*

~ John Turnipseed

Footnote for the Ego

When I have slipped on ice in the winter, I was more concerned about what other people thought than how badly I was hurt. My ego took priority over rationality. I beg you: Do not allow your ego to stop your growth through failure. If you are going to rise above your insecurities and succeed at being yourself, you can't be afraid of what other people think. Your ego must take a back seat to growth and learning.

My ratio of success versus failure has not been all that good. I would have to guess that for every success seen that there are at least one hundred failures... and even with these numbers, I may be understating.

When we look at other people's successes, we miss the stories behind them, the development, struggles, frustrations, and disappointments that came before their breakthrough. We often believe that for others, success came easy and that is far from the truth.

"Men succeed when they realize that their failures are the preparation for their victories."

~ Ralph Waldo Emerson

Gratitude for Everything

Throughout our lives there are inevitable times when things are difficult, painful and downright unfair. Being grateful can do amazing things. Gratitude reminds us to reflect and consider all that is good in our lives, no matter how small the good may appear. The experiences we encounter throughout our lives have played and will continue to play significant roles in forming who we become.

When you take the time to honour those moments, paying special attention on the growth that they facilitated, you are consciously accepting them. Through this consciousness, you can better appreciate the insights that can be extracted from even a terrible occurrence, allowing you the strength of purpose to move forward.

Taking time to reflect helps you gain new insight from past mistakes. Applying the knowledge from even the most foolish of errors gives meaning to that failure. As you appreciate the moment of enlightenment, you will gain even more wisdom along your complex journey. How you evolve through your painful experiences sets the pattern for how you handle what you must repeat. There is wisdom and healing in thankfulness.

The proverb, "Every cloud has a silver lining," shares a deep wisdom: Every negative situation has something positive within it. The positive is the silver lining. Once we get into the habit of looking for the silver lining, the cloud will not distress us as it once did.

A Tiny Bit of my Gratitude List:

Grateful to have fought the simple battles in life; giving me the ability to fight the larger ones!

Grateful to have lived in a garage over a winter, this helped revealed to me how much we can live without. Added bonus: Never take for granted the value of indoor plumbing.

Grateful to have survived and risen above abuse; creating within me the strength needed to help others who do not yet have the strength.

Grateful to have the learning disability of dyslexia; forcing me to learn many different ways of understanding.

Grateful for my near death experience; knowing that much more is waiting for us all once this journey is done.

Grateful for my difficult pregnancies; realizing the complete miracle of life.

Grateful to have been kicked out of a church; realizing that the judgment that we pass to others does not make for a better world.

Grateful to have had some close calls in life; reminding me that there are no guarantees as to how long we have and that we should live every moment as if it were our last.

Grateful to have raised two strong minded young adults;

giving me the needed moments of reflection on how little I know and how grateful I am for that.

Grateful to have failures in business; showing me how small things can change things from wrong to right.

Grateful for the need for continuous learning; No matter how hard a fall may appear, I have within me the capability to get back up, dust myself off and move forward. With the new understanding I gained, I don't need to repeat a failure. I have learned that I can move on to more explorations and lessons while continuing the cycle of life.

Grateful for my 21 years with my daughter Amber; I am thankful that my heart can be broken; for within the pain I know I have truly loved.

Grateful for my son Michael who has shown me how everyone deserves to learn their own lessons and that we all deserve to live the life we choose.

Grateful for the opportunity to share my failures with you; I am truly humbled and extremely grateful to be able to share my lessons, creating a ripple effect of acceptance and appreciation for so-called failure.

The next page are the words that I wrote on my daughters Face book page a few months after her passing. These words express my deep gratitude for having shared in her life…

Dear Amber,

I am one of the luckiest women alive because I shared 21 years with you, Amber (What an incredible spirit!) As one of your parents, I grew, I evolved, I transformed due to your strength of character.

When you were alive I was SoOo thankful that I could help you...to give to you and to teach you. However, after you finished this life here on earth, I saw how you had given back to me 'far more' than I had ever given.

Things that I had not fully recognized while you were here...

You taught me trust when you spread your wings to fly.
You taught me significance through your unconditional love.
You taught me absolute friendship through your transparency.
You taught me openness when you stood by your convictions.
You taught me to receive through your generosity
You taught me honesty when you needed guidance.
You taught me to love through your vulnerability.
You taught me patience through your kindness.
You taught me resilience through your passing.

You taught me to live life to its fullest!

Thank you Amber...

Love forever,
  Momma :)

Trial and Error

I challenge everyone to take this life and love it! Do not waste it on regrets. Grow from the life lessons which you have endured. Share your experiences. Let's merge our knowledge that we have gained from our combined failures, moving forward.

It's my hope that you'll choose to see the positive in your mistakes, setbacks, and failures. Appreciate their concealed benefits during your process of growing.

Successful people will fail more because they are doing more; progressing, moving forward, not staying in the same spot. As we look at the life-stories of amazing achievers, we find each one faced tremendous discouragement and setbacks on the way to higher levels of success. Rising to greatness is not an easy task.

The success that has been attained by others has been attained through failure; not in absence of it.

Learn to manage failure and success for this is the cycle of life. Make failure your friend. When you change your paradigm about a set outcome, good or bad, you open yourself up for reflection, then knowledge and then wisdom.

Do not be too concerned about being completely on track when you set a specific goal. Remain focused on the basic direction that you're traveling. Remain committed to that goal while still remaining flexible enough to alter your path when failure surfaces... and it will! These are qualities that are necessary for moving forward in life.

What is right or wrong for one is not necessarily right or wrong for another. Your specific path does not matter. The key is to adjust your plans as you progress through the process of failure. This adjustment happens when you take the experience and turn it into knowledge. You will face both positives and negatives in your journey.

The majority of times, your first attempt to accomplish what you set out to achieve is slim to none. You will grow through failure in your journey to success. Why not embrace this fact and stop fighting the most natural course of life, which is failure?

If at first you don't succeed, stay focused on your goals, continuing to learn and grow through them. Whatever you do, do NOT give up!

As you continue forward, allow the process to guide you. You will certainly become stronger. This strength will permit you to handle the future bumps, moving forward. Reaching your goals is not a matter of wishing. Reaching your goals requires passion. From your passion take action to move forward to your success.

Thomas Edison is a brilliant example of one who did not allow failure to stop him. He failed more than 10,000 times before creating the light bulb but he chose to view it as part of the process.

If you don't allow failure to enter into the equation, you are closing many doors to endless possibilities. Be honest with yourself: Ask yourself, how many times am I willing to fail on the road to success?

Colonel Sanders, the founder of Kentucky Fried Chicken (KFC), was rejected more than 1,000 times while attempting to sell his recipe before he finally received a *yes*.

Taking action without any backup plans sets up only two possible outcomes: The first is what we call success, which means having achieved our goal and the second is not achieving our goal. We tend to view this as failure but we should not. Instead, we need to view this outcome as guidance while we re-think, re-route, and continue on.

When you are ready to take action, you also need to be prepared for failure, accepting the guidance which comes from not getting things right the first time. What you do with your new found wisdom determines your future success. So, how *do you* or *should you* deal with failure?

We are the artist and designer of the tapestry of our lives. Once we can understand and appreciate that every circumstance, mistake, crisis and dilemma can be a learning situation, we become free from these negative labels.

The lessons that are not learned are doomed to repeat themselves until we finally get the message. When we realize that everything we do contains the seeds of knowledge within it, we will become more relaxed in even the most difficult setbacks.

My intention in sharing my challenges and weaknesses is to help reflect a world of celebrated imperfection. My hope is that you do not have to hit the wall of unknowing in order to know. However, if that is where you are headed or where you have come from, please remember: Everything is for the greater purpose of your personal enlightenment.

In admitting failure we have successfully failed, and it is then...no longer failure!

Beyond Failure

"To laugh often and much;

To win the respect of intelligent people and the affection of children;

To earn the approbation of honest critics and endure the betrayal of false friends;

To appreciate beauty;

To find the best in others;

To give of one's self;

To leave the world a bit better, whether by a healthy child, a garden patch, or a redeemed social condition;

To have played and laughed with enthusiasm and sung with exultation;

To know even one life has breathed easier because you have lived

This is to have succeeded."

~ *Ralph Waldo Emerson*

Great Examples of Failure

Leo Tolstoy flunked out of college. He was described as both unable and unwilling to learn, yet he wrote some of the greatest fiction the world has ever known.

Louisa May Alcott, author of *Little Women*, was encouraged to find work as a servant by her family because they didn't believe that she would amount to anything.

Emily Dickinson had only seven poems published in her lifetime.

18 publishers turned down **Richard Bach's** submission. Macmillan finally published *Jonathan Livingston Seagull* in 1970. By 1975 it had sold more than 7 million copies in the U.S. alone.

21 publishers rejected **Richard Hooker's** humorous war novel, *M*A*S*H*.

27 publishers rejected **Dr. Seuss's** first book, **Jack London** received six hundred rejection slips before he sold his first story.

English crime novelist, **John Creasey,** received 753 rejection slips before he published 564 books.

Gertrude Stein submitted poems to editors for nearly 20 years before one was finally accepted. *"A Rose is a Rose is a Rose."*

A Paris art dealer refused **Picasso** shelter when he asked if he could bring in his paintings from out of the rain.

Rodin's father once said, "I have an idiot for a son." Described as the worst pupil in the school, he was rejected three times admittance to the Ecole des Beaux-Arts. Many museums are now named after the sculptor of *The Thinker*.

Oprah Winfrey was fired from her first television job as an anchor in Baltimore, where she said she faced sexism and harassment.

Harrison Ford's first performance as a hotel bellhop in the film *Dead Heat on a Merry-Go-Round*, the studio vice-president dismissed Ford with, "You ain't got it kid, you ain't got it ... now get out of here."

Michael Caine's headmaster told him that he would be a labourer all of his life.

Charlie Chaplin was initially rejected by Hollywood studio chiefs because his pantomime was considered nonsense.

Steven Spielberg was rejected by the Southern California University of Cinematic Arts multiple times.

In February 1962, Decca Records rejected **The Beatles** because they sounded too much like the **Shadows** and that such guitar groups were on the way out.

At one audition he was told he couldn't sing, another said he had no ear for harmony, while another told him he'll never make it as a singer, yet **Elvis Presley** is widely known as *The King of Rock and Roll*.

Beethoven was totally deaf by the time when he wrote his famous Ninth Symphony. He attached a special nob to the soundboard of his piano which he could bite and sense the vibration of his music. At the end of the premiere performance, he had to be turned around to see the tumultuous applause of the audience. Hearing nothing; he wept.

Walt Disney was fired by a newspaper editor because, "He lacked imagination and had no good ideas." He went bankrupt several times before he built Disneyland. The proposed park was rejected by the city of Anaheim on the grounds that it would only attract riffraff.

Charles Schultz had every cartoon he submitted rejected by his high school yearbook staff but went on to create *Charlie Brown*.

After his first audition, **Sidney Poitier** was told by the casting director, "Why don't you stop wasting people's time and go out and become a dishwasher or something?" It was at that moment, recalls Poitier, that he decided to devote his life to acting.

When **Lucille Ball** began studying to be an actress in 1927, she was told by the head instructor of the John Murray Anderson Drama School, "Try any other profession."

Winston Churchill suffered from a speech impediment requiring speech therapists. He is one of the most famous leaders and orators ever. His inspirational speeches are often quoted. In his first speech as Prime Minister he declared, "I have nothing to offer but blood, toil, tears, and sweat."

Sigmund Freud was booed from the podium when he first presented his ideas to the scientific community of Europe. He returned to his office and kept on writing.

Charles Darwin gave up a medical career and was told by his father, "You care for nothing but shooting, dogs and rat catching."

In his autobiography, Darwin wrote, "I was considered by all my masters and my father, a very ordinary boy, rather below the common standard of intellect."

Thomas Edison's teachers said he was, "Too stupid to learn anything." He was fired from his first two jobs for being, *"non-productive."* As an inventor, Edison made 1,000 unsuccessful attempts at inventing the light bulb. When a reporter asked, *"*How did it feel to fail 1,000 times?"

Edison replied, "I didn't fail 1,000 times. The light bulb was an invention with 1,000 steps."

Albert Einstein did not speak until he was 4-years-old and did not read until he was 7. His parents thought he was *sub-normal* and one of his teachers described him as, "Mentally slow, unsociable, and adrift forever in foolish dreams." He was expelled from school and was refused admittance to the Zurich Polytechnic School. He did eventually learn to speak and read, even to do a little math.

Louis Pasteur, world renowned microbiologist, was only a mediocre pupil in undergraduate studies and ranked 15th out of 22 students in chemistry.

Henry Ford, founder of Ford Motor Company, failed and went broke five times before he succeeded.

R. H. Macy failed seven times before his store in New York City caught on.

F. W. Woolworth was not allowed to wait on customers when he worked in a dry goods store because, his boss said, "He didn't have enough sense."

When **Bell telephone** was struggling to get started, its owners offered all their rights to Western Union for $100,000. The offer was disdainfully rejected with, "What use could this company make of an electrical toy?"

Rocket scientist, **Robert Goddard,** found his ideas bitterly rejected by his scientific peers on the grounds that rocket propulsion would not work in the rarefied atmosphere of outer space.

Daniel Boone was once asked by a reporter if he had ever been lost in the wilderness. Boone thought for a moment and replied, "No, but I was once bewildered for about three days."

An expert said of **Vince Lombardi**: "He possesses minimal football knowledge and lacks motivation."

Lombardi would later write, "It's not whether you get knocked down; it's whether you get back up."

Michael Jordan was cut from his high school basketball team. Jordan once observed, "I've missed more than 9000 shots in my career. I've lost almost 300 games. Twenty-six times I've been trusted to take the game winning shot and missed. I've failed over and over and over again in my life. And that is why I succeed."

Babe Ruth hit 714 home runs and struck out 1,330 times in his career. "Every strike brings me closer to the next home run."

Hank Aaron went 0 for 5 his first time at bat with the Milwaukee Braves.

Stan Smith was rejected as a ball boy for a Davis Cup tennis match because he was too awkward and clumsy. He went on to clumsily win Wimbledon and the U.S. Open and eight Davis Cups.

Tom Landry, Chuck Noll, Bill Walsh, and **Jimmy Johnson** accounted for 11 of the 19 Super Bowl victories from 1974 to 1993. They also share the distinction of having the worst records of first-season head coaches in NFL history.

After **Carl Lewis** won the gold medal for the long jump in the 1996 Olympic Games, he was asked to what he attributed his longevity, having competed for almost 20 years. He said, "Remembering that you have both wins and losses along the way. I don't take either one too seriously."

The Key to Success… is Failure!

Insights on Failure

"History has demonstrated that the most notable winners usually encountered heart-breaking obstacles before they triumphed. They won because they refused to become discouraged by their defeats."

~ B.C. Forbe

"Making your mark on the world is hard. If it were easy, everybody would do it. But it's not. It takes patience, it takes commitment, and it comes with plenty of failure along the way. The real test is not whether you avoid this failure, because you won't. It's whether you let it harden or shame you into inaction, or whether you learn from it; whether you choose to persevere."

~ Barack Obama

"I am not judged by the number of times I fail, but by the number of times I succeed; and the number of times I succeed is in direct proportion to the number of times I can fail and keep on trying."

~ Tom Hopkins

"Keep in mind that our community is not composed of those who are already saints, but of those who are trying to become saints. Therefore let us be extremely patient with each other's faults and failures."

~ Mother Teresa

"The best way out is always through."
~ Robert Frost

"It's fine to celebrate success but it is more important to heed the lessons of failure."
~ Bill Gates

"The first step toward success is taken when you refuse to be a captive of the environment in which you first find yourself."
~ Mark Caine

"Most people give up just when they're about to achieve success. They quit on the one yard line. They give up at the last minute of the game, one foot from a winning touchdown."
~ Ross Perot

"A life spent making mistakes is not only more honourable but more useful than a life spent in doing nothing."
~ George Bernard Shaw

"Every failure brings with it the seed of an equivalent success."
~ Napoleon Hill

"Failure will never overtake me if my determination to succeed is strong enough."
~ Og Mandino

"Failures, repeated failures, are finger posts on the road to achievement. One fails forward toward success."

~ C. S. Lewis

"Do the one thing you think you cannot do. Fail at it. Try again. Do better the second time. The only people who never tumble are those who never mount the high wire. This is your moment. Own it."

~ Oprah Winfrey

"I've come to believe that all my past failure and frustrations were actually laying the foundation for the understandings that have created the new level of living I now enjoy."

~ Tony Robbins

"I didn't fail 10,000 times. The light bulb was an invention with 10,000 steps."

~Thomas Edison

Printed in Great Britain
by Amazon